BOOK OF
Lists II

By James Buckley, Jr.
and
Robert Stremme

SCHOLASTIC

an imprint of

SCHOLASTIC

D1055759

Produced by Shoreline Publishing Group LLC
Santa Barbara, California
www.shorelinepublishing.com
Editorial Director: James Buckley, Jr.
Designed by Tom Carling, www.carlingdesign.com.
Illustrations by Chip Wass and Steckfigures, Inc.
Additional editorial help provided by
Beth Adelman (copy, additional text), Nanette Cardon (index),
and Jim Gigliotti (additional text).
Thanks to Danny Biederman (www.spyfiarchives.com) for the cool list on page 180.

Thanks to the awesome Paula Manzanero (and the "geniuses in production") at Scholastic
for putting up with wayward authors and laughing at all (well . . . most) of Jim's jokes.

Library of Congress Cataloging-in-Publication Data
    Buckley, James, 1963–
        Scholastic book of lists II / James Buckley, Jr. and Robert Stremme.
          p. cm.
        Includes index.
        ISBN 0-439-83763-4
          1. Handbooks, vade-mecums, etc.—Juvenile literature. I. Stremme, Robert. II. Title.
        III. Title: Scholastic book of lists two. IV: Title Scholastic book of lists 2.

        AG106.B83 2007
        031.02—dc22

                          2006050591

Printed in the United States
First printing, September 2007

Table of Contents

Introduction

We're back! Did you miss us? We had so much fun making the first *Scholastic Book of Lists* — and so many of you had so much fun reading it — we decided to make another one! And so . . . welcome to the second entry on the list of *Scholastic Books of Lists*!

In the first *Book of Lists*, we covered a lot of the basics: presidents, oceans, Super Bowl winners, bones, baby animals, popular magazines, blah, blah, blah. Well . . . been there, done that! In this all-new edition, we've packed it with tons of really fun lists that will _____ you. (Please fill in the blank with one or more words from the following list of verbs.)

- thrill
- amaze
- stun
- entertain
- surprise
- startle
- tickle
- bother

As you can see, we just love lists. They're so handy and compact. They're so easy to organize and remember. They're so easily recognized by readers. They're so, well . . . cute! (Okay, maybe not the one on page 226 — your call.)

In this new edition of

the *Scholastic Book of Lists*, you'll find all sorts of new, cool stuff. Knights (page 16) and days (page 253). Ups ("Shuttle Stuff," page 111) and downs (deepest caves, page 98). Garth Brooks (page 170) and famous cooks (page 242). We pass on gas (page 129) and hit a Homer (page 192). We've got La La and Ya Ya (page 207) and ha-ha (depending on your point of view, page 272). We've got niblicks and pharaohs and bivalves, oh my!

In this new edition, we've added a chapter all about food, so you can make your own list of what you'd like to use to "soup up" (see page 225) your school lunch menus. Look for tasty things like cow brain tacos, lobster ice cream, marigolds, and silkworm grubs! Mmm, mmm, good!

Oh, yes, indeed, there is a world of interesting info jam-packed into these colorful pages. Do you know what octophobia is? Check out page 254 (but don't look at the page to the left if you've got it . . . aaaah!).

> In various places throughout this book, you'll see boxes like this one. Here's where we'll try to ask — and answer — questions that might pop up in our minds (and, we hope, yours) about some of the info on the page. You might also see an exclamation point. It's all in an effort to add cool background stuff, contribute to the vast spread of knowledge, or just try to squeeze in a few more jokes.

Can you name the world's stinkiest plant (and no, it's not your sibling's socks)? Hold your nose and read page 133. Do you know who actually cheers for banana slugs? Why, some of my best friends do, and you can see why on page 292.

You can even find out where Chargoggagoggmanchauggagoggchaubunagungamaugg is located.

So, does all this sound like more homework? Well, it's not. And to prove it, we've even put in some games, one at the end of each chapter, to let you have even more fun. Read over the lists, have fun with the games (the answers begin on page 318 if you want to cheat!), and make a list of all the things you like about the book. No matter how you use the book, remember: You're number one on our list.

Abbreviations Used in This Book

Most of the abbreviations used are for measurements. We're using both the "regular" American system and the metric system (read more about them on page 116).

C	Celsius	l	liter	sq. mi.	square
F	Fahrenheit	lb.	pound		mile
ft.	foot	m	meter	tbs.	tablespoon
g	gram	oz.	ounce	tsp.	teaspoon
kg	kilogram	sq. km	square	yd.	yard
km	kilometer		kilometer		

CHAPTER ONE

History

Just because stuff happened before you were born doesn't mean it isn't important! So, our present to you is a trip to the past.

History Periods

Scientists look at history in a different way than the rest of us. While we're busy trying to memorize dates (1492, 1776, etc.) or figure out who came first, the Romans or the Greeks, or to remember who won the Battle of the Bulge, paleontologists and other scientists are looking way, way, way, way back in the fossil record. They divide time not in mere years, but in "ages," "periods," "epochs," "eons," and other lengthy time periods. Here's a list, in order of most recent to oldest, of the "periods" into which history is divided by science. (Note: Some of the specific years noted might vary from source to source.)

NAME	MILLIONS OF YEARS AGO
Quatenary	today to 1.8
Tertiary	1.8–65
Cretaceous	65–146
Jurassic	146–208
Triassic	208–248
Permian	248–280
Pennsylvanian	280–325
Mississipian	325–360
Devonian	360–408
Silurian	408–438
Ordovician	438–505
Cambrian	505–540
Vendian/Ediacaran	540–600

Columbus Came Later

Was Columbus the first guy to set foot in North America? Nope. Though his journey in 1492 was important to the eventual settling (or conquering, depending on your point of view) of the Americas, he was far from the first. People had been living there for thousands of years. Here's a list of some civilizations living far from Europe before the time of Columbus.

North America

Thousands of Native American tribes, too numerous to list here, including those existing today and some that have disappeared, were living in what is now the United States and Canada.

Central America

The major civilizations included Aztec, Huastec, Maya, Mixtec, Olmec, Pipil, Tarascan, Teotihuacán, Toltec, Totonac, and Zapotec.

South America

Large civilizations or tribes included Chavín, Chibcha, Chimor, Chachapoya, Huari, Inca, Moche, Nazca, Tairona, and Tiawanaku.

Was Columbus Even First?

Many experts think that Vikings were actually the first to reach North America, perhaps in about A.D. 1000. Some stories say that Chinese explorers reached the West Coast before Columbus arrived in the east. There are also some scholars who say sailors from the Islamic Empire or traders from West Africa arrived in North America as much as 500 years before ol' Christopher. Columbus got his own day and lots of nice statues, but the debate about him goes on.

GREAT
World Empires

For many centuries, the world was organized not by nations, but by empires. One group of people — usually led by one strong leader — conquered large swaths of territory, creating empires that stretched for thousands of miles. Of course, you couldn't vote to become part of an empire; it was pretty much decided for you. Empires rose and fell over the centuries, expanding into new areas and carrying their cultures with them. Here's a list of some of the most important or prominent . . . and here's hoping we don't see any new ones any time soon. (Note: The dates are approximate; they didn't all have starting and ending times like a movie or a modern country; for the most part, they grew slowly and faded over time.)

EMPIRE (LOCATIONS)	APPROX. DATES
Egyptian (Egypt/N. Africa)	**3000 BCE–30 BCE**
Greek (Europe/Middle East/N. Africa)	**1500 BCE–150 BCE**
Roman (Europe/Asia/N. Africa)	**600 BCE–410**
Macedonian* (Middle East/Asia)	**330 BCE–310 BCE**
Han (China)	**200 BCE–220**
Byzantine (Middle East/Asia)	**400–1450**

Arab/Islamic (Europe/Africa)   630–1250

Ghana (West Africa)   800–1200

Mongol# (India/Asia)   1100–1360

Inca (Central South America)   1200–1550

Mali (West Africa)   1250–1400

Ottoman (Middle East/Central Asia)   1300–1918

Songhay (West Africa)   1400–1590

Aztec (Mexico)   1420–1530

Hapsburg (Europe)   1430–1800

British (Worldwide)   1550–1940

Soviet (Eastern Europe/Central Asia)   1917–1991

*This was the empire of Alexander the Great, the Greek-trained Macedonian warrior who in a very brief time created one of the largest empires ever.

#Genghis Khan was the main leader of this Asiatic empire.

Good Knights!

In olden times, English knights earned their spurs with great deeds on the battlefield. Monarchs chose them and rewarded them with lands and manors and all that cool stuff. Knights today are also chosen by the British monarch, but they are honored for their work in many areas far from the battlefield. Most are British citizens, but the queen can choose to award honorary knighthoods to folks from elsewhere. Here's a list of people awarded knighthoods; they can't officially be called Sir, but it's nice to know someone thinks they're worthy of it!

Bono, Irish rock star and activist

George H. W. Bush, former U.S. president

Placido Domingo, Italian opera singer

Bill Gates, U.S. business leader

Bob Geldof, Irish musician and fund-raiser

Billy Graham, U.S. preacher

Alan Greenspan, U.S. economist

Rudolph Guiliani, U.S. politician

Pelé, Brazilian soccer star

Steven Spielberg, U.S. moviemaker

Donald Tsang, Hong Kong politician

Simon Wiesenthal, Israeli writer

Knights of the Round Table

Knights often appear in fiction, too. The most famous are the Knights of the Round Table, from the many legends about the British King Arthur. Sir Thomas Malory, a writer in the 1400s, popularized the stories of the Round Table, but parts of it contain much older legends. The knights themselves had many adventures, and while none are as well-known as Arthur, they're still worthy of getting their own list. Here are the main guys who sat around the Round Table. (Some of the names are spelled in different ways in different retellings.)

Sir Bedevere	Sir Galahad	Sir Gereaint	Sir Lancelot
Sir Bors	Sir Gareth	Sir Kay	Sir Percival
Sir Gaheris	Sir Gawain	Sir Lamorak	Sir Tristan

Princess Power!

Though there are dozens of real-life princesses around the world today, they don't wear those pointy hats you see in old paintings, they rarely live in tall towers, and they are never threatened by dragons. However, they are indeed princesses — the daughters of kings and queens or other princes and princesses, or the wives of princes. Only a few belong to royal families that actually rule their countries, but that doesn't mean that every little girl in those countries doesn't look up at the princesses and sigh. . . . Here are few of the world's current princesses.

Belgium
Mathilde, Elisabeth, Astrid, Luisia Maria, Maria Luisa, Maria Laura, Laetitia Maria, Claire, Louise

Burundi
Esther

Denmark
Mary, Alexandra, Benedikte, Elisabeth

Great Britain
Anne, Beatrice, Eugenie, Sophie

Japan
Masako, Aiko, Kako, Mako, Hanako, Yuriko, Tonahito, Akiko, Yohko, Takamado, Yasuko, Akishino, Mikasa

Liechtenstein
Marie Aglae, Sophie, Marie-Caroline, Tatjana, Maria-Annunciata, Marie Astrid, Marie Caroline

Luxembourg
Alexandra

Monaco
Caroline, Stéphanie, Andrea, Charlotte,
Alexandra

Morocco
Lalla Salma, Lalla Asma, Lalla Hasna,
Lalla Meyrem

Netherlands
Máxima, Catharina-Amalia, Alexia, Laurentien,
Mabel, Eloise, Lenore

Norway
Mette-Marit, Ingrid Alexandra, Martha Louise,
Maud, Leah

Romania
Margarita

Russia
Olga, Xenia

Spain
Letizia, Leonor, Elena, Cristina

Sweden
Victoria, Madeleine

Uganda
Elizabeth

Arrr! Pirates!

Thanks to that guy from the Caribbean, pirates are hot again. For centuries (most famously in the 1500–1700s), they were more than hot – they were starting fires . . . and looting ships and sacking towns and capturing prizes and all that piratical stuff. They were not really nice, after all, and their main job was pretty much breaking every law they could. Some of them gained more fame than others. Here's a list of some real-life (that is, *not* Johnny Depp) pirates.

Blackbeard Perhaps the best-known pirate ever, his real name was Edward Teach. In a wild-and-woolly two-year career, he wrecked dozens of ships and built a reputation for real ferocity.

Anne Bonny Along with her friend Mary Read, Anne was that rarest of people: a female pirate. Sailing on the ship of Calico Jack, she and Jack fought – and went to prison – like other pirates.

Cheng Chiu-Long and Cheng I Sao This pair of Chinese pirates sailed separately, but caused plenty of damage. Cheng I Sao was one of the few woman pirate captains.

William Kidd One of the most famous pirates ever, Capt. Kidd began his pirating career, like Henry Morgan, with permission to sack enemy ships. He soon moved away from this legal career to a full-blown life as a pirate.

Jean Lafitte This Louisiana-based French pirate turned (temporarily) from criminal to American patriot, helping defeat the British in the Battle of New Orleans during the War of 1812.

Henry Morgan A British captain, he was at first given permission to attack the enemy Spanish . . . but he kept on attacking even after England and Spain made peace!

Black Bart Roberts Another British pirate, he supposedly captured more than 400 ships in his pirating career.

Named for . . .

You got your name from your parents, and you probably got to name your pets. But who names states? In some cases, states were named by settlers for something "back home" (New York, New Jersey, New Hampshire). Some places honor famous people in Europe: Maryland (Queen Mary), Georgia (King George), the Carolinas (King Charles). However, the names of the majority of states come from a name the land had already, often given by a Native American group (they were here first, after all). Here's a look at what some of those Native American names mean in their original languages.

STATE (NATIVE NATION)	**MEANING**
Alaska (Aleutian)	"Land that is not an island"
Arizona (Aztec)	"Silver-bearing"
Connecticut (Mohican/Algonquin)	"Long river place"
Illinois (Illini/Algonquin)	"Warriors"
Kansas (Sioux)	"South wind people"
Kentucky (Iroquois)	"Land of tomorrow"
Michigan (Chippewa)	"Great water"
Minnesota (Dakota Sioux)	"Sky-tinted water"
Mississippi (Chippewa)	"Great river"
Missouri (Algonquin)	"River of the big canoes"
North and **South Dakota** (Sioux)	"Friend"
Ohio (Iroquois)	"Fine river"
Tennessee (Cherokee)	Tanasi, name of native village
Utah (Shoshone/Navajo)	"Higher up"
Wyoming (Algonquin)	"Large prairie place"

Fathers of . . .

Officially, a man can only be the father of a son or daughter. But that hasn't stopped history from making guys the fathers of all sorts of things. They might have been the inventor or developer of an idea or product, the first leader of a country or a movement, or the person who made something popular. George Washington is the "Father of our country," for example. However they got the title, they're all "Fathers of . . ." the following things.

FATHER	OF
Kemal Ataturk	Turkey*
Stephen Austin	Texas
Alexander Graham Bell	Telephone
Tim Berners-Lee	World Wide Web
Nolan Bushnell	Computer games
Vinton Cerf	The Internet
Louis Daguerre	Photography
Sigmund Freud	Psychoanalysis
Mohandas Gandhi	Modern India
Giuseppe Garabaldi	Modern Italy
Robert Goddard	Rocketry
W.C. Handy	The Blues
Jim Henson	The Muppets
Gugliemo Marconi	Radio
Karl Marx	Communism
Sir John MacDonald	Canada
Robert Oppenheimer	Atomic bomb
Fr. Junipero Serra	California
Igor Sikorsky	Helicopter
Otto von Bismarck	Modern Germany
John Wanamaker	Department stores

*The nation, not the bird.

Mothers of . . .

Don't worry, we won't leave moms out! Here's a list, similar to the one on page 22, that features women who have gone down in history for being so important to an invention, country, or cause that they are called the "Mother of . . ." But how many of these things do you think send a card on Mother's Day?

MOTHER/OF

Jane Addams/Social work

Isadora Duncan/Modern dance

Mary "Mother" Jones/Community activism

Florence Nightingale/Modern nursing

Dorothy Page/Iditarod dogsled race

Rosa Parks/Civil rights movement

Betsy Ross/United States flag

Mary Shelley/Science fiction

Winnie Mandela/South Africa

? Did she or didn't she? That is, did Betsy Ross *really* sew the first American flag? The legend says that in 1777 she was approached by several people, including George Washington, to sew a new design for a "stars and stripes" flag for the soon-to-be nation. Some facts bear out the legend, but ultimately, we may never know for sure.

LOST Civilizations

How can you lose a civilization? You can lose a sock or lose a moment or lose a tooth . . . but a civilization? Well, sadly, it's happened a few times in history. Due to disease or war or drought or just the effects of time, some hearty and healthy civilizations have either disappeared or been swallowed up by others and become just a memory. Plus, there's one on this list that really is just a myth . . . but we thought we'd toss it in there anyway in case you've seen it lying around somewhere.

Anasazi Native American tribe in Southwest U.S. that "vanished" in about 1300.

Angkor Wat Built in the 1100s in what is now Thailand by a now-gone civilization, these temples were lost for hundreds of years before being "found" again in 1860.

Atlantis Mentioned in only a couple of ancient histories, this island nation supposedly sank beneath the waves thousands of years ago.

Babylon A large civilization in Mesopotamia conquered and abandoned by the Greeks in 312.

Cahokia/Mississipian At its peak in the 1200s, the Native American city of Cahokia was the biggest in North America; about 200 years later, it was empty.

Pompeii One day in 79, a thriving city-state in Italy. The next, a smoldering heap of ash after Mt. Vesuvius erupted and destroyed the place.

Troy Though there is some disagreement about whether this place was real or not, a site in Turkey is thought by many to have been Troy, site of Homer's *Iliad*, a story about the Trojan War.

World's Fairs

Since the late 1700s, enormous exhibitions called World's Fairs have thrilled millions. The high point of World's Fairs was the three or four decades before World War I. At the Fairs, the host nations put out examples of the many wonderful things in that country. Other countries then constructed large pavilions to do the same. Before the age of air travel and TV, World's Fairs were a great way for people to "see" the world. These days, Fairs are fewer . . . but they're still fun. Here's a list of the last 10 World's Fairs, plus a list of some World's Fairs held in the United States.

Recent World's Fairs

YEAR	LOCATION
2008	Zaragoza, Spain (scheduled)
2005	Aichi, Japan
2002	Switzerland (several cities)
2000	Hanover, Germany
1998	Lisbon, Portugal
1993	Taejon, South Korea
1992	Genoa, Italy
1992	Seville, Spain
1988	Brisbane, Australia
1986	Vancouver, Canada

World's Fairs in United States Since 1940

1984	New Orleans, La.
1982	Knoxville, Tenn.
1974	Spokane, Wash.
1968	San Antonio, Tex.
1964	New York, N.Y.
1962	Seattle, Wash.
1942	Los Angeles, Calif.
1940	Los Angeles, Calif.

Phamous Pharaohs

In the ancient land of Egypt, the pharaoh was the top cat. Revered as a human god by his (or her) people, pharaohs ruled over Egypt for thousands of years. A few of them stand out from the dusty sands of history as more accomplished or more renowned. Dates shown are the middle of their reigns.

Sneferu, c. 2600 BCE
Built several of the famous pyramids that still stand in Egypt

Khufu, c. 2575 BCE
Builder of the Great Pyramid of Egypt

Khafra, c. 2540 BCE
Erected the famous statue of the Sphinx

Hatshepsut, c. 1490 BCE
An early female pharaoh, she expanded Egypt's trade.

Amenhotep III, c. 1375 BCE
Another great builder, he put up several key monuments.

Akhenaten, c. 1360 BCE
Tried to get his people to believe in one god instead of many

Tutankhamun, c. 1330 BCE
Not a superstar pharaoh, but his tomb is the best preserved ever found

Ramses II, c. 1250 BCE
Great warrior who defeated the enemy Hittites

Cleopatra, c. 50 BCE
One of only a few female pharaohs

Kids in Charge!

You have to be at least 35 years old to be president of the United States. However, age was no barrier to the kids on this list. They were all (at least in name) the rulers of their countries. Not a bad job if you can get it!

RULER	FIRST YEAR	AGES*
Baldwin V, King of Jerusalem	1177	0–9
Margaret I of Scotland	1283	0–7
Louis XVII of France	1785	0–9
King John I of France	1316	0–5 days
Alfonso XI, King of Leon (in Spain)	1312	1
King Fuad II of Egypt	1952	1
Henry Pu Yi, Emperor of China	1909	3–6
Christina of Sweden	1632	5
Leo II, Byzantine emperor	474	7
James II of Scotland	1437	7
Tutankhamun, Pharaoh of Egypt	1333 BCE	8–18
Edward VI of England	1546	9–16

*Ages in years during time they were in charge, which started in the year listed. Some of them lived longer than their reigns lasted.

In Their Packs

The explorers William Clark and Meriwether Lewis were charged by President Thomas Jefferson to check out the Louisiana Purchase, the newest part of the United States. Jefferson had bought the land from France and wanted to know more about what he had just bought! To make this journey, which began in 1804, Lewis and Clark had to assemble an enormous list of supplies. We don't have room to list all of them, but here are some of the smaller, handy items the two men might have put in their own backpacks at some point during the journey.

✔ **Books** (on things like botany, navigation, minerals, etc.)

✔ **Chronometer** (a type of watch helpful in navigation)

✔ **Fishing hooks, fishing line** (for catching food, of course)

✔ **Pocket mirrors, beads, ivory combs, silk ribbons** (taken as presents for natives)

✔ **Rush's pills** (medicine for indigestion)

✔ **Soap** (yes, believe it or not, they actually washed once in a while)

✔ **Steels** (pieces of metal used to make sparks and thus, fire)

✔ **Stockings** (socks . . . you can never have enough dry socks!)

✔ **Surveyor's compass** (to help them make maps)

✔ **Telescope** (it's a big place, the West)

✔ **Thermometer** (for the water and the air, not the men)

✔ **Tobacco** (they didn't know that smoking or chewing is bad for you)

✔ **Tools** (such as pliers, chisels, needles, etc.)

✔ **Whetstone** (for sharpening knives)

FAMOUS
Frontiersmen

Pull on your buckskins, grab a chaw of jerky, and take a seat 'round the campfire. It's time to take a look at these here wild 'n' woolly fellas what helped tame the West (most in the early and mid-1800s). Afeared of nuthin', they hacked into the wilderness in search of furs, gold, or jest adventure. See ya around down the trail, tenderfoots!

Jim Beckwourth One of the few African-American mountain men, he was an explorer and soldier.

Jim Bowie Texas legend, fighter, soldier, and rancher

Jim Bridger Fur trapper, explorer, and all-around mountain man

Kit Carson Fur trapper who became key guide for John Fremont and was later a famous soldier

Buffalo Bill Cody Began as a buffalo hunter, became the greatest showman in the West

Davy Crockett Explorer and soldier, he found time between adventures to serve in Congress!

John C. Fremont Soldier who led exploration of the West, especially California

Hugh Glass Explorer who once made a 200-mile walk after being mauled by a bear

Jedidiah Smith Famed for his journeys into uncharted areas, especially the Southwest

Patriot Days

Key Battles of the American Revolution

Well, we wouldn't be here without them! These are the key battles fought between British and Colonial forces during the Revolutionary War. Also listed are the states (as of today) that were the sites of the battles.

BATTLE (STATE)	YEAR
Lexington/Concord (Mass.)	1775
Bunker Hill (Mass.)	1775
Long Island (N.Y.)	1776
White Plains (N.Y.)	1776
Trenton (N.J.)	1776
Germantown (Penn.)	1777
Saratoga (N.Y.)	1777
Monmouth (N.J.)	1778
Charleston (S.C.)	1780
King's Mountain (S.C.)	1780
Yorktown (Va.)	1781

Merci!

The final battle of the war came when about 8,800 soldiers of the Continental Army under Gen. George Washington bottled up British forces near Yorktown, Va. They were aided by more than 10,000 French troops, who landed behind the British. On October 19, 1781, Gen. William Cornwallis officially surrendered.

Us vs. Us

Major Battles of the Civil War

The Civil War was the costliest war in American history, with more Americans dying or being wounded than in any other conflict. The main reason? Americans fought on both sides as Union states fought to keep Confederate states from leaving the United States. Here's a list of the major battles in the Civil War, including the states in which they were fought.

BATTLE (STATE)	YEAR
Fort Sumter (S.C.)	1861
First Battle of Bull Run (Va.)	1861
New Orleans (La.)	1862
Second Battle of Bull Run (Va.)	1862
Antietam (Md.)	1862
Fredericksburg (Va.)	1862
Chancellorsville (Va.)	1863
Vicksburg (Tenn.)	1863
Gettysburg (Penn.)	1863
Chickamauga (Ga.)	1863
Battle of the Wilderness (Va.)	1864
Atlanta (Ga.)	1864
Appomattox Surrender (Va.)	1865

World War I

From July 1914 to November 1918, the world was at war. Battles between Allied forces (led by Great Britain, France, and, later, the United States) and forces of the German and Austrian Empires raged in Europe, Asia, Africa, and the Middle East. It was called "the war to end all wars," a statement that has, sadly, proven to be quite false. There's no way to include all the events of the war on this list, but here's a quick overview of the most important battles and events.

1914

Aug.: Austria invades Serbia, while Germany invades Luxembourg, Belgium, France, and Prussia. In response, Great Britain joins the war to defend allies such as France.

Aug. 30: Battle of Tannenberg; Germany defeats Russian forces advancing on Germany from the east.

Sept.: First Battle of Marne (France) fought between Allied forces and German troops.

Nov.: First Battle of Ypres (Belgium) was the first real "trench warfare" battle, using what would become the signature strategy of the war.

Nov.: Turkey joins the war on the side of Germany.

1915

Jan.: Germany becomes the first to use poison gas in battle.

Jan. 19: For the first time, German airships, called *Zeppelins*, fly over and bomb England.

May: Second Battle of Ypres.

May 7: Germany sinks the passenger ship *Lusitania*.

Fall–Winter: Several major battles result in huge casualties, but little strategic movement.

1916

Feb.: Battle at Verdun (France).

May: Battle of Jutland between Allied and German naval forces; no clear winner.

July–Nov.: The Allied attack becomes the Battle of the Somme in France.

1917

April: Spurred by evidence of German designs on North America via Mexico, and seeing the trouble Allied forces were in, U.S. president Woodrow Wilson declares war against Germany and its allies.

May: First American troops arrive in France.

July–Nov.: Third Battle of Ypres, as Allied forces, aided by the Americans, push against German positions.

1918

July: Germany makes another attack at another Battle of the Marne (France), but can't break through.

Aug.: British and Canadian troops drive the Germans back to the Hindenburg Line, their final line of retreat toward Germany.

Nov. 9: Seeing defeat ahead, Kaiser Wilhelm II of Germany resigns.

Nov. 11: On 11/11/18, at 11:11 A.M., documents are signed that end the "war to end all wars."

So how did it all start? Well, like most things about wars, it's complicated. However, there was one event that triggered it (or that some countries used as a trigger), and that was when Archduke Franz Ferdinand of Austria was killed on June 28, 1914, in Sarajevo by Gavrilo Princip. The Austrians blamed Serbia (among others) and declared war a few months later. That started the dominos falling and World War I was raging soon after.

World War II

About 20 years after being defeated in World War I, Germany rose up again as a power in Europe. Led by the Nazi dictator Adolf Hitler, Germany invaded neighboring countries and allied with the equally land-hungry Japanese empire. World War I had been wide-ranging, but World War II was even bigger, with armed battles on almost every continent. Like World War I, it's hard to gather into a list, but we'll give it a try with these key events.

1939

Sept.: Germany invades Poland, and Great Britain and France declare war on Germany to defend Poland.

1940

Spring: German forces roar through and take over Belgium, Netherlands, Denmark, Norway, and France.

May: British forces are driven out of Europe at Dunkirk, France, evacuating with help from hundreds of private boats.

Fall: Battle of Britain fought in the air above England, as British air forces mark a huge victory.

1941

Jan. 21: The battle moves to Africa, as Allied forces battle Germans at Tobruk in the German colony of Libya.

June 22: Germany invades the Soviet Union; soon after, it takes over Greece and Yugoslavia.

Fall: Japan invades neighboring countries, including China, the Philippines, and Indonesia.

Dec. 7: Japan bombs U.S. naval base at Pearl Harbor, Hawaii. The United States declares war on Japan and its ally Germany.

1942

Spring: Japan continues its march in the Pacific, taking Singapore, Java, Borneo, and Sumatra.

June: U.S. naval forces defeat the Japanese at the Battle of the Midway in the Pacific Ocean.

Fall: Germany's African forces fall to British troops at the Battle of El Alamein.

1943

Feb.: American forces recapture the island of Guadalcanal, while British troops attack in Burma.

Feb.: Soviet forces defeat German forces at Stalingrad in the first major defeat of Germany.

Sept.: Italy is invaded from North Africa by Allied forces, resulting in the surrender of Italy, a key Germany ally.

1944

June 5: A month after a major invasion at Anzio, Italy, Rome is recaptured from German forces by Allied armies.

June 6: D-Day, the invasion of German-controlled Europe by Allied forces.

July: American forces retake the Pacific island of Guam from Japan.

Aug.: Paris is freed of German control for the first time since 1940.

Dec.: The Battle of the Bulge is fought as Germany tries to counterattack.

1945

Jan.: Allied forces retake the Philippines.

Spring: German V1 and V2 rocket bombs continue to land in England.

April 21: After a race through Germany by the Allied and Soviet armies, Soviet forces are the first to reach the German capital of Berlin.

May 7: Germany surrenders; Hitler commits suicide.

Aug.: U.S. plane drops atomic bombs on Hiroshima and Nagasaki, Japan, the first (and still only) used in combat.

Aug. 14: Japan surrenders.

ALMOST President

Every book of lists has the list of U.S. presidents. That's an easy list to make, though. This book goes one step further into the obscure world of American history. Here's a list that doesn't include the guys who won the election for president . . . this is a list of the guys who came in *second*!

YEAR	PRESIDENTIAL RUNNER-UP
2004	John Kerry
2000	Al Gore
1996	Bob Dole
1992	George H. W. Bush
1988	Michael Dukakis
1984	Walter Mondale
1980	Jimmy Carter
1976	Gerald Ford
1972	George McGovern
1968	Hubert Humphrey
1964	Barry Goldwater
1960	Richard M. Nixon
1956	Adlai Stevenson
1952	Adlai Stevenson
1948	Thomas Dewey
1944	Thomas Dewey
1940	Wendell Wilkie
1936	Alf Landon
1932	Herbert Hoover
1928	Al Smith
1924	John Davis
1920	James Cox
1916	Charles Hughes
1912	Theodore Roosevelt

YEAR	PRESIDENTIAL RUNNER-UP
1908	William Jennings Bryan
1904	Alton Parker
1900	William Jennings Bryan
1896	William Jennings Bryan
1892	Benjamin Harrison
1888	Grover Cleveland
1884	James Blaine
1880	Winfield Hancock
1876	Samuel Tilden
1872	Thomas Hendricks
1868	Horace Seymour
1864	George McClellan
1860	John Breckinridge
1856	John C. Fremont
1852	Winfield Scott
1848	Lewis Cass
1844	Henry Clay
1840	Martin Van Buren
1836	William Henry Harrison
1832	Henry Clay
1828	John Quincy Adams
1824	John Quincy Adams
1820	John Quincy Adams
1816	Rufus King
1812	DeWitt Clinton
1808	Charles Pinckney
1804	Charles Pinckney
1800	Aaron Burr*
1796	Thomas Jefferson
1792	John Adams
1788	John Adams

*Burr actually tied Thomas Jefferson with 73 Electoral College votes apiece. The election was decided by the House of Representatives.

Gearin' Up
A Bicycle Time Line

Cavemen didn't have 'em, Socrates never saw one, Columbus didn't ride one, and George Washington was stuck with a horse. What were they all missing out on? Bicycles! Here's a quick rundown on how the modern bicycle was developed.

1817 Germany's Karl Drais created a two-wheeled contraption that a person could "ride" by sitting on it and just walking.

1860s The "boneshaker" became a hit. The model made by Pierre Michaux of France was popular; it had spinning pedals that turned the hard wheels directly, without a chain.

1870 James Starley created the penny farthing, a bike with an enormous front wheel. The rider sat as much as eight feet (2 m) above the ground!

1885 Starley's nephew John created the Rover, a bike that looked much more like today's. Its diamond-shaped frame featured a chain, pedals, a more comfortable seat, and handlebars. This became known as the "safety bike" model.

1888 Inflatable tires were first used; whew! Before then, tires were solid, so you can imagine that the ride was not too smooth!

1890s Invention of coaster brakes, hand brakes, and gears. Before then: no brakes . . . no gears!

1970 First BMX bike track opened in California.

1979 Gary Fisher starts the first "mountain bike" company, creating a whole new class of bikes.

Revvin' Up
An Automobile Time Line

It's hard to believe, but less than a century ago, more people got around on horses than in cars. Today, of course, there are about as many cars in the United States as there are people, and there's almost no place on the planet you can go without having to look both ways before your cross the street. Where did they all come from? Here are some key milestones in the early history of automobiles. Start your engines!

1862 Étienne Lenoir of France created the first gasoline engine. He tried it on a wagon (after unhitching the horse, of course) and went 12 miles (19 km). Then he forgot all about it and worked on motorboats.

1876 German engineer Nicholas Otto created a type of gasoline engine known as a "four-stroke." It became the model for all future engines.

1885 Karl Benz (yep, the future Mercedes-Benz guy) was the first person to combine a gas engine with a frame and wheels to make . . . ta-dah! . . . a motor car.

1891 Charles Duryea made the first cars in America. Eight years later, Random Olds (later of "Oldsmobile" fame) opened the first car factory in America.

1908 Henry Ford introduced the Model T, the first mass-produced car.

1918 Ford creates the first pickup truck model.

1937 The first versions of the Volkswagen Beetle hit the road in Germany; it would become one of the world's bestselling car models, with more than 21 million sold.

1957 Japanese cars (Toyotas) enter the American market.

1997 In Japan, the Toyota Prius becomes the first mass-produced gas-electric hybrid car.

U.S. Female Firsts

Someday in the future, it won't matter when a woman does something for the first time. It will just be another day and another event. But until then, we celebrate women who, through the years, have overcome all sorts of obstacles. Today, women can expect to be just about anything they want, but for many centuries in America, that wasn't the case. Here's a list of some notable "firsts" by women in history.

Jane Addams
First American woman to win the Nobel Peace Prize, 1931

Madeline Albright
First female Secretary of State, 1997

Elizabeth Blackwell
First female American doctor, 1849

Anne Bradstreet
First American woman to publish a book, 1650

Pearl S. Buck
First American woman to win Nobel Prize for literature, 1938

Amelia Earhart
First woman pilot to cross the Atlantic solo, 1932

Geraldine Ferraro
First woman nominated by major party (Democratic) for vice president, 1984

Carly Fiorina
First woman to head one of nation's top 50

corporations (Hewlett-Packard), 1999

Lucy Hobbs
First female dentist, 1866

Wilma Mankiller
First woman chief of major Native American nation (Cherokee), 1985

Arabella Mansfield
First American woman lawyer, 1869

Jerrie Mock
First woman to fly around the world by herself, 1964

Sandra Day O'Connor
First female Supreme Court justice, 1981

Joanne Pierce and Susan Roley
First female FBI agents, 1972

Harriet Quimby
First female licensed pilot in U.S., 1911

Jeannette Rankin
First female congressperson (Montana), 1917

Janet Reno
First female U.S. attorney general, 1993

Libby Riddles
First woman to win the famous Iditarod dogsled race in Alaska, 1985

Mary Walker
First (and still only) woman to win the Congressional Medal of Honor, 1865

Then vs. Now

Looking back a century or so, the biggest changes from then to now are the ones that folks back then barely considered: computers, the Internet, world jet travel, space flight, and television, among others. But there are quite a few things we can compare in American life from in or around 1907 to today.

SUBJECT	C. 1907	C. 2007
U.S. population	87 million	300 million
U.S. federal budget	$579,000,000	$2.7 trillion
Number of cars	8,000	200 million
Miles of paved roads	10	4 million
Auto deaths	97	43,000
Speed limit (mph)	15	65
Life expectancy (years)	47.3	77.5
Average worker's pay	$13/week	$788/week
Toy fad	Teddy bears	Yu-Gi-Oh!
Newish popular sport	Ping-Pong	Parkour
Homes with telephones	7 percent	99 percent

SUBJECT	C. 1907	C. 2007
Homes with bathtubs/ showers	14 percent	96 percent
Homes with TVs	0 percent	98.2 percent
Height of flight	Wright Bros.	Space shuttle
Number of states	46*	50
Number of farms	5.7 million	2 million
Forms of energy	Coal 74% Wood 23%	Oil 40% Gas 24% Coal 21%
Music heroes	Irving Berlin George M. Cohan	Jesse McCartney P. Diddy
National college football champ	Yale	Florida#
World Series champ	Chicago Cubs	St. Louis Cardinals#
First-class stamp	$0.02	$0.39
Dozen eggs	$0.14	$1.50
Pound of butter	$0.24	$2.25

*Oklahoma became the 46th state in 1907.
#2006 season champ

History
Game Page

We'll start you off with a two-part game. First, fill in the missing years in the questions. Then find the answers in the grid at the bottom. They'll be in the grid vertically or horizontally, not diagonally, but might be backward or upside-down! The answers to the questions should be found in this History chapter.

1. In what year did World War I end? _____

2. The most recent World's Fair in America was held in _____.

3. When did the Devonian age begin (in mya)? _____

4. In what year did Barry Goldwater finish second in the race for president? _____

5. When did Montenegro become an independent country? _____

6. In what year was the Battle of Saratoga? _____

7. When did the battle at Fort Sumter happen? _____

8. When did the first BMX bike track open? _____

9. In what year did Amelia Earhart fly across the Atlantic solo? _____

10. In what year was the D-Day invasion? _____

1	1	9	8	7	4	0	7	1	1	3	4
2	3	9	1	3	2	8	5	8	1	0	1
8	1	9	8	4	0	4	2	6	7	1	9
9	8	7	4	5	1	2	3	1	9	8	1
1	8	9	4	0	9	6	6	0	1	9	8
1	9	4	4	7	9	2	0	1	4	3	0
9	1	4	5	8	0	9	6	7	7	7	1
7	4	0	3	5	8	1	9	6	4	2	9
0	6	0	0	2	8	3	6	5	0	1	0

44

CHAPTER TWO

Social Studies

Go to a state fair, be president, live in a castle, visit a national landmark, or have more money than anyone else in the world. Can't do all that? No problem. Just read this chapter and do all that and more.

Not Just States

The United States has 50 states, but there are places in the world that are also under the control of the United States or are supported by it. The people who live in these places are not U.S. citizens, but they do have some local control of their government. Commonwealths, for example, have a much closer relationship with the United States, including having representatives in Congress.

U.S. Territories

American Samoa
Baker Island
Guam
Howland Island
Jarvis Island
Johnston Atoll
Kingman Reef
Midway Islands
Navassa Island
Palmyra Atoll
U.S. Virgin Islands
Wake Islands

U.S.-Affiliated Commonwealths

Northern Mariana Islands
Puerto Rico

How can these places become actual states? The U.S. Congress would have to vote to make them a state and their citizens must agree via a vote. Only Puerto Rico stands a chance at this point of ever becoming a state.

AMERICAN Awards

United States military medals, such as the Purple Heart and the Silver Star, are pretty well-known. However, Congress and the president have established other medals and awards to honor outstanding achievements in fields such as the sciences, arts, and humanities. Here's a list of some of them — good luck!

Congressional Gold Medal or Medal of Honor

Honors individuals, institutions, or events for singular acts of exceptional service and for lifetime achievement. Established in 1776.

Enrico Fermi Award

Honors scientific and technological achievement in the development, use, control, or production of energy. Established in 1956.

National Humanities Medal

Honors individuals and organizations for their notable contributions to the humanities. Established in 1988, this award was called the Charles Frankel Prize until 1996.

National Medal of Arts

Honors artists and supporters of the arts for outstanding contributions to the arts (visual, musical, theatrical, etc.) in the United States. Established by the National Endowment for the Arts and the president in 1985. Up to 12 medals may be awarded each year.

National Medal of Science

Honors individuals for their work in physics, biology, mathematics, engineering, and the social and behavioral sciences. Established in 1959, it has been awarded by the National Science Foundation and the president since 1962.

National Medal of Technology

Honors individuals, groups, or companies for contributions to economic, environmental, and social well-being through technology. Established in 1980.

Presidential Medal of Freedom

Honors exceptional meritorious service and is the nation's highest civilian award. Established by President Harry S. Truman in 1945.

Island Countries

An island is a landform that is completely surrounded by water. There are hundreds of thousands of islands around the world, but only these 48 are independent countries. Let's hope all their inhabitants know how to swim. . . .

Antigua and Barbuda

Australia

Bahamas

Bahrain

Barbados

Cape Verde

Comoros

Cuba

Cyprus

Dominica

East Timor

Fiji

Grenada

Iceland

Indonesia

Ireland

Jamaica

Japan

Kiribati

Madagascar

Maldives

Malta

Marshall Islands

Mauritius

Micronesia

Nauru

New Zealand

Palau

The Philippines

St. Kitts and Nevis

St. Lucia

St. Vincent and the Grenadines

Samoa

São Tomé and Príncipe

Seychelles

Singapore

Solomon Islands

Sri Lanka

Taiwan

Tonga

Trinidad and Tobago

Tuvalu

United Kingdom

Vanuatu

Own Your Own Island

Perhaps the title of this list should be "Have Lots of Money and Own Your Own Island." With enough money, you can own an island in its wild, natural state or an island ready to be filled with buildings and people. Have fun shopping!

ISLAND	LOCATION	COST (millions of dollars)
James Island	Canada	$49
Isla de sa Ferradura	Spain	$39
Keswick Island	Australia	$33
Koro Island	Fiji	$27.5
Sultan's Island	Indonesia	$27.5
Blue Lagoon Island	Fiji	$25
Isle of St. John	USA (Florida)	$25
Koh Fan Noi and Koh Fan Yai	Thailand	$24
Little Ragged Island	Bahamas	$24
Thatch Cay	St. Thomas	$24
Haapiti Nui Island	French Polynesia	$18

Got Island?

Believe it or not, it's pretty easy to find an island to buy (if you've got the money!). Several companies represent people trying to buy and sell islands. One Web site has a quiz you can take to see if island living is for you. One question asks what you like to do on vacation . . . another asks what you would do if your toilet overflows!

Famous Castles

Castles bring up images of knights, drawbridges, and battles, but many castles are just home sweet home. They are called castles because of their size and architecture. This list of world castles includes both military castles and castle homes. You can visit many of them, such as Bran Castle (legendary home of Count Dracula) and Neuschwanstein (the model for many fairy-tale castles).

CASTLE	COUNTRY
Alhambra	Spain
Amber Fort	India
Blair Castle	Scotland
Blarney Castle	Ireland
Bran Castle	Romania
Cardiff Castle	Wales
Castel del Monte	Italy
Edinburgh Castle	Scotland
Le Mont St. Michel	France
Lismore Castle	Scotland
Kremlin	Russia
Laquila Castle	Italy
Heidelberg Castle	Germany
Himeji Castle	Japan
Gondar Castles	Ethiopia
Mysore Palace	India
Neuschwanstein	Germany
Nijo Castle	Japan
Red Fort	India
Tower of London	England
Versailles	France
Windsor Castle	England

They've Struck Oil

Oil: The whole world needs it to do everything from power cars to heat homes, but not every country has its own supply. The future of energy may include greater use of solar, wind, and nuclear power, but until those are more plentiful, here are the places the world will look to get the oil it needs.

COUNTRY/OIL RESERVES (billion barrels)

Saudi Arabia/**262**

Canada/**179**

Iran/**126**

Iraq/**115**

Kuwait/**102**

United Arab Emirates/**98**

Venezuela/**77**

Russia/**60**

Libya/**39**

Nigeria/**35**

? Oil is measured in barrels, not gallons. How much oil is in one barrel? Most experts use a standard of 42 gallons (190 l) to equal one barrel (though, to make matters more confusing, the standard barrel used to ship oil holds 55 gallons/250 l). One barrel of oil is the same as 224 cans of soda. Two million barrels of oil (or so) would fill a football stadium.

WORLD'S BUSIEST
Airports

Someone really does count the passengers flying in and out of airports! This list includes the airports that have the most passengers going through them each year, listed in order of busiest. Also, the list shows the home city and three-letter code that is used around the world for each airport; learn the secret language of airlines!

Hartsfield-Jackson Atlanta International Airport
(ATL) Atlanta, Georgia

O'Hare International Airport
(ORD) Chicago, Illinois

Heathrow Airport
(LHR) London, England

Haneda Airport
(HND) Tokyo, Japan

Los Angeles International Airport
(LAX) Los Angeles, California

Dallas/Fort Worth International Airport
(DFW) Dallas, Texas

Charles de Gaulle Airport
(CDG) Paris, France

Frankfurt Airport
(FRA) Frankfurt, Germany

Amsterdam Airport Schiphol
(AMS) Amsterdam, Netherlands

Denver International Airport
(DEN) Denver, Colorado

McCarran International Airport
(LAS) Las Vegas, Nevada

Phoenix Sky Harbor International Airport
(PHX) Phoenix, Arizona

CITIES WITH Subways

Subway cars chug through tunnels beneath more than 90 cities around the world. London has the oldest subway, opened in 1863. Boston was the first city in the United States to have a subway system, in 1898. Ten U.S. cities now have systems that include some or all underground trains.

Subways in the United States

Atlanta	Miami
Baltimore	New York City
Boston	Philadelphia
Chicago	San Francisco
Los Angeles	Washington, D.C.

Busiest Subways Around the World

Moscow	Paris
Tokyo	Osaka
Seoul	London
Mexico City	Hong Kong
New York City	St. Petersburg

Cleveland, Ohio, began building a subway system in 1920 and finally stopped construction in 1948 — without finishing it. Many of the stations and tunnels still exist under the city, but the system never opened.

HAPPY BIRTHDAY,
States!

Happy birthday to each of the 50 United States! They are listed here in the order in which they became states. Feel free to send them a card. Also listed is the year in which their state quarter — a specially designed 25-cent coin — was or will be issued as part of a 10-year program from the U.S. Mint. Collect 'em all!

STATE	DATE OF STATEHOOD	QUARTER ISSUE
Delaware	December 7, 1787	1999
Pennsylvania	December 12, 1787	1999
New Jersey	December 18, 1787	1999
Georgia	January 2, 1788	1999
Connecticut	January 9, 1788	1999
Massachusetts	February 6, 1788	2000
Maryland	April 28, 1788	2000
South Carolina	May 23, 1788	2000
New Hampshire	June 21, 1788	2000
Virginia	June 25, 1788	2000
New York	July 26, 1788	2001
North Carolina	November 21, 1789	2001
Rhode Island	May 29, 1790	2001
Vermont	March 4, 1791	2001
Kentucky	June 1, 1792	2001
Tennessee	June 1, 1796	2002
Ohio	March 1, 1803	2002
Louisiana	April 30, 1812	2002
Indiana	December 11, 1816	2002
Mississippi	December 10, 1817	2002

Illinois	December 3, 1818	2003
Alabama	December 14, 1819	2003
Maine	March 15, 1820	2003
Missouri	August 10, 1821	2003
Arkansas	June 15, 1836	2003
Michigan	January 26, 1837	2004
Florida	March 3, 1845	2004
Texas	December 29, 1845	2004
Iowa	December 28, 1846	2004
Wisconsin	May 29, 1848	2004
California	September 9, 1850	2005
Minnesota	May 11, 1858	2005
Oregon	February 14, 1859	2005
Kansas	January 29, 1861	2005
West Virginia	June 20, 1863	2005
Nevada	October 31, 1864	2006
Nebraska	March 1, 1867	2006
Colorado	August 1, 1876	2006
North Dakota	November 2, 1889	2006
South Dakota	November 2, 1889	2006
Montana	November 8, 1889	2007
Washington	November 11, 1889	2007
Idaho	July 3, 1890	2007
Wyoming	July 10, 1890	2007
Utah	January 4, 1896	2007
Oklahoma	November 16, 1907	2008
New Mexico	January 6, 1912	2008
Arizona	February 14, 1912	2008
Alaska	January 3, 1959	2008
Hawaii	August 21, 1959	2008

In Our Cabinet

This list of jobs in the U.S. government includes the titles of the people who run important national departments, a group called the Cabinet. These folks are appointed by the president and confirmed by the Senate. They can be replaced at any time. When a president leaves office, the Cabinet traditionally resigns so the new president can appoint his or her own people.

Cabinet Positions

Secretary of State
Secretary of the Treasury
Secretary of Defense
Attorney General
Secretary of the Interior
Secretary of Agriculture
Secretary of Commerce
Secretary of Labor
Secretary of Health and Human Services
Secretary of Housing and Urban Development
Secretary of Transportation
Secretary of Energy
Secretary of Education
Secretary of Veterans Affairs
Secretary of Homeland Security

Cabinet-Level Positions

These officials may attend cabinet meetings.

Vice President of the United States

White House Chief of Staff

Deputy Chief of Staff

Administrator of the Environmental Protection Agency

Director of the Office of Management and Budget

Director of the National Drug Control Policy

U.S. Trade Representative

Director of the CIA

United States Ambassador to the United Nations

Under Secretary of Homeland Security for
   Emergency Preparedness and Response

White House Counsel

National Security Advisor

Director of National Intelligence

Stick Around

How long we will live is determined by many factors — some we can control and some we can't. The country in which you live is one of the most important factors. Swaziland has the lowest life expectancy (the number of years most people can be expected to live, based on the average of all the people in the country), at 33.2 years. Life expectancy in the United States is 77.7 years. These 15 countries have the highest life expectancies.

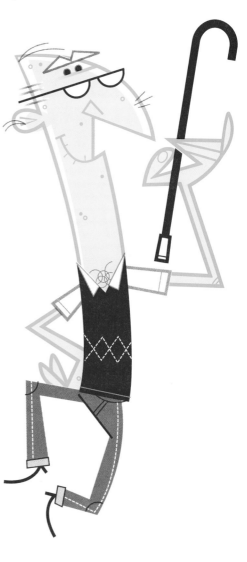

COUNTRY	LIFE EXPECTANCY (YRS.)
Andorra	83.5
San Marino	81.6
Singapore	81.6
Japan	81.2
Switzerland	80.4
Sweden	80.4
Australia	80.4
Iceland	80.2
Canada	80.1
Italy	79.7
France	79.6
Spain	79.5
Monaco	79.5
Liechtenstein	79.5
Norway	79.4

Spending Our Money

Your parents have a household budget — that is, how much money they make balanced against how much your family has to spend on stuff you all need. Budgets can vary a lot, depending on your family. But no matter how rich your family is, the United States federal budget works with much bigger numbers. In this list, the numbers represent billions (with a big, giant, green *B*) of dollars. Our federal government collects and spends huge amounts of money.

The Money Comes In

SOURCE (IN BILLIONS)

Individual income taxes	$1,167
Social Security contributions	911
Corporate income taxes	243
Excise taxes	79
Miscellaneous	50
Estate/gift taxes	24
Customs, duties	32

The Money Goes Out

EXPENSE (IN BILLIONS)

Social Security	$600
National defense	466
Medicare	412
Income security	374
Health	302
Net interest	272
Education, social services	85
Transportation	73
Veterans' benefits	73
Justice administration	42
International affairs	37
Natural resources, environment	30
Commerce, housing	30
Science, space, technology	25
Agriculture	20
General government	18
Community/regional development	15

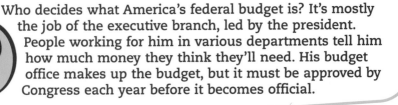

Who decides what America's federal budget is? It's mostly the job of the executive branch, led by the president. People working for him in various departments tell him how much money they think they'll need. His budget office makes up the budget, but it must be approved by Congress each year before it becomes official.

Before They Were Prez

If your future career plans include being President of the United States, check out this list of some pre-president occupations. Lots of presidents were governors or lawyers before they got into politics. But some took other paths to the White House. Sure, you can be a lawyer and then be president. Then again, you could also be a tailor or a wool carder. Is this a great country or what?

George Washington	Surveyor, soldier, farmer
Thomas Jefferson	Farmer, governor, inventor, diplomat
Andrew Jackson	Soldier, farmer
William Henry Harrison	Soldier
Zachary Taylor	Soldier
Millard Fillmore	Wool carder apprentice
Andrew Johnson	Tailor
Ulysses S. Grant	Soldier, farmer, store clerk
James A. Garfield	Teacher, preacher, soldier
Chester A. Arthur	Teacher, engineer
Theodore Roosevelt	Rancher, soldier
Woodrow Wilson	Teacher, university president
Warren G. Harding	Newspaper editor
Herbert Hoover	Mining engineer
Harry S. Truman	Farmer, shopkeeper, soldier
Dwight D. Eisenhower	Soldier, university president
John F. Kennedy	Soldier, author
Lyndon Johnson	Teacher, rancher
Jimmy Carter	Engineer, soldier, farmer
Ronald Reagan	Sports announcer, actor
George H. W. Bush	Soldier, ambassador, CIA director
George W. Bush	Oil company executive, baseball team owner

THE FIRST **President** TO ...

Our country has been governed by many presidents. As history and technology have changed the world, the presidents have changed and adapted the office of the president. Here is a fun list of some important (and some silly) presidential firsts.

First President to . . .

George Washington ... Be president (duh!), plus have a pilot's license for a hot air balloon

John Adams ... Live in the White House, then called the President's House

Thomas Jefferson ... Shake hands, not bow, when meeting people

James Madison ... Wear long pants regularly, instead of knee breeches

James Monroe ... Ride on a steamboat

John Quincy Adams ... Be photographed and write a book of poetry

Andrew Jackson ... Ride on a train

Martin Van Buren ... Be born as an American citizen (all previous presidents had been born before the Revolution as British subjects)

William Henry Harrison ... Die in office

Millard Fillmore ... Have running water and a stove in the White House

Franklin Pierce ... Be born in the 1800s

James Buchanan . . . Be a bachelor when elected

Abraham Lincoln . . . Wear a beard while in office

Ulysses S. Grant . . . Be ticketed for speeding in his horse and buggy

Rutherford B. Hayes . . . Use a telephone in the White House

James A. Garfield . . . Be left-handed

Grover Cleveland . . . Be married in the White House

Benjamin Harrison . . . Use electricity in the White House

Theodore Roosevelt . . . Ride in an airplane and a car

William H. Taft . . . Throw out the opening ball for baseball season

Franklin D. Roosevelt . . . Appear on television

Dwight D. Eisenhower . . . Ride in a helicopter

John F. Kennedy . . . Be born in the 1900s

Richard M. Nixon . . . Resign from office

Jimmy Carter . . . Be born in a hospital

Ronald Reagan . . . Appoint a woman to the Supreme Court

William Clinton . . . Have been a Rhodes Scholar

The Supremes

Nine justices sit on the Supreme Court of the United States of America. They are chosen by the president and approved by the Senate. And get this — they can keep the job the rest of their lives! They can retire, of course, but these are some of the very few U.S. government jobs appointed for life. In 2005, John G. Roberts became the 17th Chief Justice of the Supreme Court. With the appointment of Samuel Alito in 2006, there have been 110 Supreme Court justices. These are the members of the court at the end of 2006.

JUSTICE	BEGAN SERVICE	APPOINTED BY PRESIDENT
John Paul Stevens	December 19, 1975	Gerald Ford
Antonin Scalia	September 26, 1986	Ronald Reagan
Anthony M. Kennedy	February 18, 1988	Ronald Reagan
David H. Souter	October 9, 1990	George H. W. Bush
Clarence Thomas	October 23, 1991	George H. W. Bush
Ruth Bader Ginsburg	August 10, 1993	William Clinton
Stephen G. Breyer	August 3, 1994	William Clinton
John G. Roberts	September 29, 2005	George W. Bush
Samuel A. Alito, Jr.	January 31, 2006	George W. Bush

Who was the first Chief Justice of the Supreme Court? The office was created with the ratification of the U.S. Constitution in 1789. President George Washington nominated John Jay, a former foreign minister and president of the Continental Congress. The Senate confirmed Jay and he became the first Chief Justice.

Men ON THE Moon

Between 1969 and 1972, the United States sent six Apollo missions to the moon. Each time, two members of the three-man crew walked on the moon. The third man (the guy with the *) orbited the moon in the command module. (That must have been a bummer; go all the way to the moon and then not walk on it! That would be like having to stand outside and watch while your friend ate in an ice-cream shop!)

APOLLO 11
JULY 1969

Neil Armstrong
Edwin Aldrin
Michael Collins*

APOLLO 12
NOVEMBER 1969

Charles Conrad
Alan Bean
Richard Gordon*

APOLLO 14
FEBRUARY 1971

Alan Shepard
Edgar Mitchell
Stuart Roosa*

APOLLO 15
JULY 1971

David Scott
James Irwin
Alfred Worden*

APOLLO 16
APRIL 1972

Charles Duke
John Young
Thomas Mattingly*

APOLLO 17
DECEMBER 1972

Eugene Cernan
Harrison Schmitt
Ronald Evans*

Words of Wisdom

The first words spoken on the moon came from Neil Armstrong: "That's one small step for a man, one giant leap for mankind." The last words were spoken by Eugene Cernan: "America's challenge of today has forged man's destiny of tomorrow."

Capital Ideas

Here are some fun facts about U.S. state capitals. (Vocabulary hint: *Capital* with an *a* is the geographic location; *capitol* with an *o* is the actual building that houses the state government.)

Juneau, Alaska
Named after Joseph Juneau, who discovered gold here in 1880.

Hartford, Connecticut
American Cookery, the first American cookbook, was published here in 1796.

Springfield, Illinois
Basketball was invented at the YMCA at Springfield College in 1891.

Boston, Massachusetts
At the Old Granary Burying Ground, look for Mother Goose's grave.

St. Paul, Minnesota
The capitol building was modeled after St. Peter's Basilica in Rome.

Helena, Montana
In 1864, gold was discovered at Last Chance Gulch, now Helena's main street.

Lincoln, Nebraska
Home to the world's only roller skating museum.

Columbus, Ohio
Try a hamburger at the very first Wendy's, opened in 1969.

Oklahoma City, Oklahoma
In 1935, the country's first parking meter was installed here.

Richmond, Virginia
Its capitol building was designed by a well-known architect, inventor, farmer, and president — Thomas Jefferson.

ODD NATIONAL
Landmarks

There are many famous landmarks around the United States, such as Mount Rushmore in South Dakota and the Statue of Liberty in New York City. But everyone has heard of those. Why not be a trailblazer among your friends and be the first to say you've seen these unusual national landmarks?

Crazy Horse Memorial

Located in Crazy Horse, South Dakota, this statue is being carved from a 600-foot (183 m) mountain. Begun in 1948, when finished it will depict Native American leader Crazy Horse on his horse (who, as far as we know, was not crazy).

Fountain of Youth

Tradition says that this natural spring in St. Augustine, Florida, is the Fountain of Youth sought after and "discovered" by Spanish explorer Ponce de Leon in 1513. People still drink the water to see if it works.

Four Corners marker

Colorado, New Mexico, Arizona, and Utah's borders all meet at one spot, marked by a concrete slab. When you get there, see if you can put your body in all four states at one time.

Hollywood sign

Left over from a sign that originally said "Hollywoodland," these famous letters can be seen in the hills overlooking Los Angeles, California.

London Bridge

The original London Bridge that crossed over the Thames River in England now crosses over an artificial lagoon in Lake Havasu City, Arizona.

Lucy the Elephant

Built in 1881 in Margate, New Jersey, Lucy the Elephant has been a home, a bar, and a hotel, and has hosted weddings. You can tour this 65-foot (20-m) structure and imagine what it would be like to sleep inside the belly of an elephant. Although Lucy is probably not as smelly as a real pachyderm.

Royal Roll Call

When we think about royalty, we usually think of "Once upon a time . . ." But kings, queens, sultans, emperors, sheiks, princes, and emirs still rule in some countries. Some of these royals have absolute power in their countries. Other kings and queens hold positions in constitutional governments.

COUNTRY	MONARCH (AS OF THE END OF 2006)
Bahrain	King Hamad bin Isa al-Khalifa
Belgium	King Albert II
Bhutan	King Jigme Singye Wangchuck
Brunei	Sultan Haji Hassanal Bolkiah
Cambodia	King Norodom Sihamoni
Denmark	Queen Margrethe II
Japan	Emperor Akihito
Jordan	King Abdullah II
Kuwait	Sheik Jabir al-Ahmad al-Sabah
Lesotho	King Letsie III
Liechtenstein	Prince Hans Adam II
Luxembourg	Grand Duke Henri
Malaysia	King Syed Sirajuddin
Monaco	Prince Albert II
Morocco	King Muhammad VI
Nepal	King Gyandendra
Netherlands	Queen Beatrix
Norway	King Harald V
Oman	Sultan Qabus ibn Sa'id
Qatar	Emir Sheik Hamad ibn Khalifa al-Thani
Saudi Arabia	King Abdullah
Spain	King Juan Carlos I
Swaziland	King Mswati III
Sweden	King Carl XVI Gustaf
Thailand	King Bhumibol Adulyadej
Tonga	King Tupouto
United Kingdom	Queen Elizabeth II

Are You on This List?

When a baby is born in the United States, the parents usually apply for a Social Security card and the Social Security Administration records the baby's name — so they know what names are in and what names are out! See how names have changed over a 50-year span. Are you on this list?

TOP 15 NAMES FOR BOYS		TOP 15 NAMES FOR GIRLS	
2004	**1954**	**2004**	**1954**
Jacob	Michael	Emily	Mary
Michael	James	Emma	Linda
Joshua	Robert	Madison	Deborah
Matthew	John	Olivia	Patricia
Ethan	David	Hannah	Susan
Andrew	William	Abigail	Debra
Daniel	Richard	Isabella	Barbara
William	Thomas	Ashley	Karen
Joseph	Gary	Samantha	Nancy
Christopher	Charles	Elizabeth	Cynthia
Anthony	Steven	Alexis	Donna
Ryan	Mark	Sarah	Pamela
Nicholas	Joseph	Grace	Sandra
David	Donald	Alyssa	Kathleen
Alexander	Ronald	Sophia	Carol

Rich People

We wish you the best of luck in someday finding your name on this list (put together by the money-obsessed people at *Forbes* magazine). And remember that you were inspired to earn your place by reading this book. You can send your thanks to us in the form of a large check! Thank you. P.S. Just kidding!

Top 10 Richest People in the World

		WEALTH (IN BILLIONS)	COUNTRY
1.	Bill Gates	$50	USA
2.	Warren Buffett	$42	USA
3.	Carlos Slim Helú	$30	Mexico
4.	Ingvar Kamprad	$28	Sweden
5.	Lakshmi Mittal	$23.5	India
6.	Paul Allen	$22	USA
7.	Bernard Arnault	$21.5	France
8.	Prince Alwaleed	$20	Saudi Arabia
9.	Kenneth Thomson	$19.6	Canada
10.	Li Ka-shing	$18.8	Hong Kong

Top 10 Richest People in the United States

		WEALTH (IN BILLIONS)	STATE
1.	Bill Gates	$50	Washington
2.	Warren Buffett	$42	Nebraska
3.	Paul Allen	$22	Washington
4.	Michael Dell	$17.1	Texas
5.	Sheldon Adelson	$16.1	Nevada
6.	Larry Ellison	$16	California
7.	Christy Walton	$15.9	Wyoming
8.	Jim Walton	$15.9	Arkansas
9.	S. Robson Walton	$15.8	Arkansas
10.	Alice Walton	$15.7	Texas

Rich Places

With the exception of Antarctica, billionaires live on every continent, in more than 50 countries. These are the top 20; is your favorite country on this list?

COUNTRY	NUMBER OF BILLIONAIRES
United States	371
Germany	55
Russia	33
Japan	27
United Kingdom	24
India	23
Canada	22
Turkey	21
Hong Kong	17
Brazil	16
France	14
Italy	14
Saudi Arabia	11
Mexico	10
Spain	10
China	8
Malaysia	8
Sweden	8
Switzerland	8
Israel	8

Famous Places

Most people think they can pray — if they pray — anywhere at all. However, the major faiths around the world have special places where people of those faiths gather together to worship. This list consists of some of the most famous places of worship around the world for the major world religions. Many are open to the public, so if you're in their area, look 'em up!

PLACE OF WORSHIP	LOCATION	FAITH
Al-Aqsa Mosque	Jerusalem, Israel	Islam
Angkor Wat	Siem Reap, Cambodia	Buddhism
Bahá'í House of Worship	New Delhi, India	Bahá'í
Basilica of Guadalupe	Mexico City, Mexico	Roman Catholic
Canterbury Cathedral	Canterbury, England	Anglican
Cathedral of St. Basil the Blessed	Moscow, Russia	Russian Orthodox
Cologne Cathedral	Cologne, Germany	Roman Catholic
Crystal Cathedral	Garden Grove, Calif.	Protestant
Haeinsa Temple	Gayasan Mt., S. Korea	Buddhism
Harmandir Sahib–Golden Temple	Amritsar, India	Sikhism
Holy Temple, Beit HaMikdash	Jerusalem, Israel	Judaism
Itsukushima Shrine	Miyajima, Japan	Shinto

# of Worship

PLACE OF WORSHIP	LOCATION	FAITH
Great Mosque & Kaaba	Mecca, Saudi Arabia	Islam
Laxminarayan Temple	Delhi, India	Hinduism
Masjid al-Nabawi	Medina, Saudi Arabia	Islam
Meiji Shrine	Tokyo, Japan	Shinto
Salt Lake Tabernacle	Salt Lake City, Utah	Mormon
Notre-Dame de Paris	Paris, France	Roman Catholic
St. Patrick's Cathedral	New York City	Roman Catholic
St. Peter's Cathedral	Vatican City	Roman Catholic
Swaminarayan Akshardham	Delhi, India	Hinduism
Temple of Saint Sava	Belgrade, Serbia	Eastern Orthodox
Touro Synagogue	Newport, R.I.	Judaism
Washington National Cathedral	Washington, D.C.	Episcopal
Wat Phra Chatuphon	Bangkok, Thailand	Buddhism
Westminster Abbey	London, England	Anglican

 Who is buried in Westminster Abbey? Under its stone floors, a favorite tourist spot, are people such as Isaac Newton, Charles Darwin, Geoffrey Chaucer, Charles Dickens, and Laurence Olivier.

Don't Do This in...

There's an old saying that goes "When in Rome, do as the Romans do." It means that you should respect the cultures and ways of the native people when you visit foreign lands. Things that we do here might be very offensive to people in other places, while things they expect us to do might be the last thing we think of! Here's a quick introduction to the kinds of things to consider when visiting other countries.

Most Arab countries

✗ Don't point or eat with your left hand; it is considered unclean.

✗ The thumbs-up hand motion doesn't mean "Way to go!" It's actually an insult.

China

✗ Men should never touch women in public.

✗ Avoid using big hand gestures when you talk.

✗ The number four is considered very unlucky here.

Germany

✗ Don't be late to meet someone. German people are very punctual and being late can be seen as an insult.

Guatemala

✗ You know the "okay" hand signal? Don't do that; it's considered obscene here.

✗ That limp handshake your dad teases you about would be perfectly fine in Guatemala.

India

✗ When jogging or exercising, women should always wear long pants.

✗ Never share food with anyone after it has been on your plate.

✗ Oddly, it's considered an insult to thank your host after a nice meal.

✗ Never touch anyone's head, even to pat a little kid.

Indonesia

✗ Avoid touching anything except the ground with your foot.

✗ During meals, avoid talking until everyone is finished eating.

✗ Do not eat while walking in public.

Japan

✗ Always take off your shoes before going into a home; you'll often be given slippers to wear instead.

✗ When using a bathroom, use the special bathroom-only slippers usually available.

✗ Don't blow your nose in public and especially not at a meal table.

✗ Don't leave chopsticks stuck in a bowl of rice; this is only done at funerals.

Russia

✗ Never show the sole of your shoe to anyone, even by accident.

✗ If you're wearing gloves, make sure to remove them before shaking hands.

Taiwan

✗ No winking!

Welcome to
the Club!

The United States has been an independent country since 1776, when we split from Great Britain. Countries are still becoming independent today. Here's a list of the countries that most recently joined the "club of nations," along with when they became independent. (Note: Along with the four listed here, 10 other countries were formed in 1991 with the breakup of the Soviet Union.)

NEW NATION	YEAR	WHAT IT WAS BEFORE
Montenegro	2006	Part of Serbia and Montenegro
East Timor	1999	Part of Indonesia
Palau	1994	United States Trust Territory
Czech Republic	1993	Part of Czechoslovakia
Slovakia	1993	Part of Czechoslovakia
Eritrea	1993	Part of Ethiopia
Serbia and Montenegro	1992	Part of Yugoslavia
Bosnia and Herzegovina	1991	Part of Yugoslavia
Kazakhstan	1991	Part of Soviet Union
Armenia	1991	Part of Soviet Union
Turkmenistan	1991	Part of Soviet Union
Macedonia	1991	Part of Yugoslavia

When You Grow Up

There are hundreds of colleges and universities for you to choose from . . . someday. Most have sports programs and it's easy to rank their teams — winners are number one. However, how do you rank a college or university away from the playing field? Lots of experts have their lists and ways of ranking. We looked them all over and put together this list of "institutions of higher learning," ranked on their national reputations.

UNIVERSITY	STATE
Harvard University	Massachusetts
Princeton University	New Jersey
Yale University	Connecticut
University of Pennsylvania	Pennsylvania
Duke University	North Carolina
Stanford University	California
California University of Technology	California
Massachusetts Institute of Technology	Massachusetts
Columbia University	New York
Dartmouth College	New Hampshire
Washington University in St. Louis	Missouri
University of California, Berkeley	California
Northwestern University	Illinois
Cornell University	New York
Johns Hopkins University	Maryland
Brown University	Rhode Island
University of Chicago	Illinois
Rice University	Texas
University of Notre Dame	Indiana
Vanderbilt University	Tennessee
Emory University	Georgia

Social Studies
Game Page

Fill in the missing letters in these words from inside the Social Studies chapter. Then use the letters you've filled in to spell the secret phrase at the bottom.

1. __OCIAL __E__URITY

2. AMERI__AN SAM__A

3. GIN__BURG

4. SRI LAN__A

5. HUM__N__TIES

6. S__BWAY

7. AN__OR__A

8. CAR__ER

9. HOM__LAND __ECUR__TY

10. AP__ __LO

__ __ __ __ __ __

__ __ __ __ __ __ __

__ __ __ __ __ !

CHAPTER THREE

World & Weather

Erupting volcanoes! Sky-high waterfalls!
Mountains that scrape the clouds!
The boiling hot molten center of the Earth!
All that, plus . . . how to make sandcastles!
(Hey, it can't *all* be incredibly exciting. . . .)

Start Climbing

Mountain climbers can travel all over the United States to tackle their favorite peaks. Different mountain systems present a variety of heights and challenges. If you want to climb the highest, though, Alaska is the place to go; that rocky (small *r*) mountain state has 18 of the 20 highest peaks in the United States. To be fair to other "high" states, though, we've included Alaska's top 10 and also listed the highest peaks in three other states.

MOUNTAIN PEAK/LOCATION	HEIGHT (FT.)	(M)
Mt. McKinley/Alaska	20,320	6,194
Mt. St. Elias/Alaska	18,008	5,489
Mt. Foraker/Alaska	17,400	5,304
Mt. Bona/Alaska	16,550	5,044
Mt. Blackburn/Alaska	16,390	4,996
Mt. Kennedy/Alaska	16,286	4,964
Mt. Sanford/Alaska	16,237	4,949
Mt. Vancouver/Alaska	15,979	4,870
South Buttress/Alaska	15,885	4,842
Mt. Churchill/Alaska	15,638	4,766
Mt. Whitney/California	14,494	4,418
Mt. Elbert/Colorado	14,433	4,399
Mt. Rainier/Washington	14,410	4,392

For whom was Mt. Whitney, the highest peak in the continental United States, named? California geologist Josiah Whitney. Amazingly, Mt. Whitney is just a short distance from Death Valley, the lowest point in the United States.

Start Swimming

Whether you prefer the breaststroke, the backstroke, the crawl, or just enjoy floating on your back, you want lots of room for swimming. The United States has many lakes that are big enough for everyone to enjoy the water. Here are some of the biggest, and the states they are in. Start swimming!

LAKE	AREA (SQ. MI.)	(SQ. KM)
Lake Superior/Michigan/Minnesota/Wisconsin*	31,700	82,103
Lake Huron/Michigan*	23,000	59,570
Lake Michigan/Illinois/Indiana/Michigan/Wisconsin	22,300	57,757
Lake Erie/Michigan/New York/Ohio/Pennsylvania*	9,910	25,667
Lake Ontario/New York*	7,520	19,477
Great Salt Lake/Utah	2,500	6,475
Lake of the Woods/Minnesota*	1,485	3,846
Lake Lliamna/Alaska	1,014	2,626
Lake Oahe/North Dakota/South Dakota	685	1,774
Lake Okeechobee/Florida	662	1,715
Lake Pontchartrain/Louisiana	631	1,634
Lake Sakakawea/North Dakota	520	1,345
Lake Champlain/New York/Vermont*	490	1,269
Becharof Lake/Alaska	453	1,173
Lake St. Clair/Michigan*	430	1,114

Lakes with * are partly in Canada.

LONGEST
Place Names

You can probably fit your address easily on an envelope. But imagine if you lived in one of the places listed below. You'd need a pretty danged big envelope! These are the longest place names in the world, along with what they mean in their native languages. Good luck pronouncing them!

1. Krungthepmahanakornamornratanakosinmahintarayutthayama-hadilokphopnopparatrajathaniburiromudomrajaniwesmahasathar-namornphimarnavatarnsathitsakkattiyavisanukamprasit

Full name of Krung Thep, a city in Thailand (We call this city Bangkok)/163 letters

TRANSLATION: "The great city of angles, the supreme unconquerable land of the great immortal divinity, the royal capital of nine noble gems, the pleasant city with plenty of grand royal palaces and divine paradises for the reincarnated deity, given by Indra and created by the god of crafting."

2. Tetaumatawhakatangihangakoauaotamateaurehaeaturipukapihi-maungahoronukupokaiwhenuaakitanarahu

Maori name for a hill in New Zealand/92 letters

TRANSLATION: "The place where Tamatea, the man with the big knees, who slid, climbed, and swallowed mountains, known as land eater, played his flute to his loved one." ANOTHER TRANSLATION: "The brow of the hill where Tamatea, with the bony knees who slid and climbed mountains, the great traveler, sat and played on the flute to his beloved."

3. Llanfairpwllgwyngyllgogerychwyrndrobwlllllantysiliogogogoch

Village in Wales/58 letters

TRANSLATION: "Saint Mary's Church in the hollow of white hazel near a rapid whirlpool and the Church of Saint Tysilio near the red cave."

4. El Pueblo de Nuestra Señora la Reina de los Angeles de Porciuncula

Former name of Los Angeles, Calif./55 letters

TRANSLATION: "The town of our lady the queen of angels of the little portion."

LONGEST
Names at Home

In the United States, we have some very long place names, too. Many names reflect the languages of the various people who settled in the area. The longest name (it has many spelling variations) belongs to a lake in Massachusetts. Take a deep breath before you say all 45 letters of Chargoggagoggmanchauggagoggchaubunagungamaugg.

NAME	LETTERS	STATE
Friendly Village of Crooked Creek	33	Georgia
Riverside Village of Church Creek	33	Maryland
Little Harbor on the Hillsboro	30	Florida
Orchard Point at Piney Orchard	30	Maryland
Big Thicket Creekmore Village	29	Texas
Monmouth Heights at Manalapan	29	Maryland
Winchester-on-the-Severn	24	Maryland
Dalworthington Gardens	22	Texas
Linstead-on-the-Severn	22	Maryland
Lauderdale-by-the-Sea	21	Florida
Kentwood-in-the-Pines	21	California
Vermillion-on-the-Lake	21	Ohio
Wymberly-on-the-March	21	Georgia
Washington-on-the-Brazos	21	Texas

Super Climbers

These 12 mountain climbers have joined a very special club. They each have climbed all of the world's highest mountain peaks. Notice that all 14 of these peaks (listed below) are in Asia. All are higher than 8,000 meters (26,250 feet); that's the minimum for what experts call big mountains. These super climbers are listed in the order in which they achieved this amazing feat. Messner completed his mountain-go-round in 1986.

Reinhold Messner/Italy
Jerzy Kukuczka/Poland
Ehardt Loretan/Switzerland
Carlos Carsolio/Mexico
Krzysztof Wielicki/Poland
Juan Oiarzabal/Spain
Sergio Martini/Italy
Park Young Seok/S. Korea
Hang-Gil Um/S. Korea
Alberto Inurrategui/Spain
Han Wang Yong/S. Korea
Ed Viesturs/United States

PEAK	HEIGHT (FT.)	(M)
Everest	29,035	8,850
K2	28,250	8,611
Kanchenjunga	28,169	8,586
Lhotse I	27,940	8,516
Makalu I	27,766	8,463
Cho Oyu	26,906	8,201
Dhaulagiri	26,795	8,167
Manaslu I	26,781	8,163
Nanga Parbat	26,660	8,125
Annapurna I	26,545	8,091
Gasherbrum I	26,470	8,068
Broad Peak	26,400	8,047
Gasherbrum II	26,360	8,035
Shisha Pangma	26,289	8,013

Mountains
& Chains

A group of mountains that is connected is called a mountain range. When mountain ranges are parallel to one another, they're called a mountain chain. Most people use both terms when referring to groups of mountains that are located near one another. These mountain ranges and chains are listed in order of the height of their highest mountain.

MOUNTAIN RANGE/CHAIN	HEIGHT (FT.)	(M)	CONTINENT
Himalayas	29,035	8,850	Asia
Karakoram	28,250	8,611	Asia
Kunlun Shan	25,326	7,719	Asia
Hindu Kush	25,230	7,695	Asia
Andes	22,385	6,692	South America
Elburz	18,602	5,670	Asia
Ellsworth	16,066	4,897	Antarctica
Alps	15,771	4,807	Europe
Virunga	14,787	4,507	Africa
Sierra Nevada	14,494	4,418	North America
Rocky	14,433	4,399	North America
Cascade	14,410	4,392	North America
Transantarctic	14,275	4,354	Antarctica
Sierra Madre Occidental	14,239	4,340	North America
Atlas	13,665	4,165	Africa
Taurus	12,848	3,916	Asia
Drakensberg	11,425	3,482	Africa
Sulaiman	11,295	3,443	Asia
Pyrenees	11,168	3,404	Europe

Smallest Countries
BY SIZE

Sure, the biggest country in the world is easy to find: It's Russia, which takes up 11 percent of all the land in the world. But what about the smallest countries? These are places you can literally circumambulate (Big word alert! It means to walk all the way around). The smallest country is actually completely surrounded by the city of Rome, Italy. In fact, if you add up the land areas of the first 13 countries on this list, you will still not fill the smallest U.S. state, Rhode Island.

COUNTRY	CAPITAL	AREA (SQ. MI./SQ. KM)
Vatican	Vatican City	0.2/.44
Monaco	Monaco	0.7/1.95
Nauru	Yaren District	8/21
Tuvalu	Funafuti	9/26
San Marino	San Marino	24/61
Liechtenstein	Vaduz	62/160
Marshall Islands	Majuro	70/181
St. Kitts and Nevis	Basseterra	104/261
Maldives	Male	115/300
Malta	Valletta	122/316
Grenada	St. George's	133/344
St. Vincent and the Grenadines	Kingstown	150/389
Barbados	Bridgetown	166/430
Antigua and Barbuda	St. John's	171/442
Seychelles	Victoria	175/455

Smallest Countries
BY POPULATION

Many of the countries that have the smallest amount of land also have the smallest populations. But not always. Another way of looking at population is to calculate population density, which means how many people live on an average square mile of land. That tells you how crowded some of these places really feel! For example, even though Monaco is on both of these "smallest" lists, it has the title of most densely populated country at 43,046 people per square mile (16,620 per sq. km). By comparison, the population density of the United States is 80 people per square mile (31 per sq. km). What a difference!

COUNTRY	POPULATION
Vatican	921
Tuvalu	11,636
Nauru	13,048
Palau	20,303
San Marino	28,880
Monaco	32,409
Liechtenstein	33,717
Saint Kitts and Nevis	38,958
Marshall Islands	59,071
Antigua and Barbuda	68,722
Dominica	69,029
Andorra	70,549
Seychelles	81,188
Grenada	89,502

Fun AT THE Poles

The North Pole and the South Pole are considered to be the top and bottom of our planet. At the top, the North Pole is made up of ocean and ice, while on the bottom, the South Pole is made up of land and ice. One is mostly ocean; one is a continent. Here are some fun facts about each.

The North Pole and the Arctic Region

* Pole is located at 90° north latitude.
* Ocean area is 5,440,000 sq. mi. (14,090,000 sq. km).
* A drifting polar ice cap covers the central surface of the Arctic.
* Ice cap is about 10 ft. (3 m) thick.
* Land regions include parts of Asia, Europe, and North America.
* The United States, Canada, Russia, Finland, Sweden, Norway, and Denmark all make claims to parts of the land.
* A submarine first crossed under the North Pole in 1958.
* Some native people live in the area, but the Arctic is mostly populated by researchers.

The South Pole and Antarctica

* Pole is located at 90° south latitude.
* Pole is 9,800 ft. (3,000 m) above sea level.
* Land area is 5,404,000 sq. mi. (14,000,000 sq. km).
* Ocean area is also called the Southern or Antarctic Ocean.
* Ice here equals 90 percent of the world's ice.
* Holds 70 percent of the world's fresh water.
* South Pole ice formed about 20 million years ago.
* Roald Amundsen of Norway led first group of explorers to the South Pole on December 14, 1911.
* Between 1,046 and 4,415 people – all researchers and support people – live in Antarctica, depending on the season.

Hold Your Breath

Pardon us while we wave away the smog so you can read this page. The quality of the air in major American cities is not as good as it could be. Especially in the hot summers, the levels of ozone and other less-than-pleasant chemicals in the air cause all sorts of problems. Here are the top 15 (or bottom 15, depending on your point of view) urban areas in the United States with the worst overall air quality.

AREA	STATE(S)
Los Angeles, Long Beach, Riverside	CA
Bakersfield	CA
Fresno-Madera	CA
Visalia-Porterville	CA
Merced	CA
Houston, Baytown, Huntsville	TX
Sacramento, Arden, Arcade, Truckee	CA-NV
Dallas, Fort Worth	TX
New York, Newark, Bridgeport	NY-NJ-PA-CT
Philadelphia, Camden, Vineland	PA-NJ-DE-MD
Washington, Baltimore, Northern Va.	DC-MD-VA-WV
Charlotte, Gastonia, Salisbury	NC-SC
Hanford, Corcoran	CA
Cleveland, Akron, Elyria	OH
Knoxville, Sevierville, La Follette	TN

 What is smog? The word comes from blending *smoke* and *fog*. Smog is caused mainly by engines burning gasoline or oil. Other smog-causers are paint fumes and factories that burn coal.

Types of Maps

A cartographer — a person who makes maps — would able be to make all of these kinds of maps. Some may be in the glove compartment of your family's car, and some are so specialized that you may never have heard of them. There seems to be a type of map to answer any geographical question.

TYPE OF MAPS	WHAT THEY SHOW
Physical	Land and water forms, using color
Political	Political boundaries, using color
Relief	Elevation, using shading
Topographic	Elevation of areas, using contour lines

SPECIALTY MAPS	WHAT THEY SHOW
Annual Precipitation	Precipitation in specific areas during the year
Climate	Weather, rainfall, fronts
Economic	Natural and manmade resources
Energy	Distribution and use of types of energy
Ethnic	Distribution of ethnic groups of people
Historical	Land and water features from past views
Languages	Languages spoken in specific areas
Mineral	Location of specific minerals
Natural Hazards	Location of storm paths, volcanoes, earthquakes, etc.
Orthophoto	Land areas, using photographs
Population	Density of people, animals in specific areas
Poverty	Distribution of wealth among people in an area
Railroad	Railroad lines
Road	Highways, roads, distances, railroads, points of interest
Time Zone	Earth divided into the 24 time zones
Vegetation	Distribution of vegetation, from tropical to desert regions
Water Resources	Available fresh water in the area
Waterways	Location and depth of all waterways

Line 'em Up

Our globes and maps are crisscrossed by lines of latitude and longitude. They help us pinpoint exact locations on the globe, using measurements called degrees (symbol: °). Each degree of latitude and longitude can be divided into 60 minutes (symbol: '), and each minute can be divided into 60 seconds (symbol: "). When using latitude and longitude, the latitude is always listed first.

Lines of Latitude Facts

- Latitude lines measure north and south, from 0° to 90°.
- The lines are an equal distance from one another, about 69 miles (110 km) apart.
- Latitude lines never touch or cross other latitude lines.
- 0° latitude is also called the Equator and is not north or south.
- 23.5° north latitude is called the Tropic of Cancer.
- 23.5° south latitude is called the Tropic of Capricorn.
- The area between the Topic of Cancer and the Tropic of Capricorn is the Tropic Zone.
- 66.5° north latitude is called the Arctic Circle.
- 66.5° south latitude is called the Antarctic Circle.

Lines of Longitude Facts

- Longitude lines, also called meridians, measure east and west from 0° to 180°.
- The lines are vertical and are widest apart at the Equator.
- 0° longitude is also called the Prime Meridian.
- 0° latitude crosses 0° longitude in the Atlantic Ocean off the west coast of Africa.
- 180° longitude is also called the International Date Line.
- The 24 time zones follow longitude lines, changing one hour for every 15°.

Are We Here Yet?

See the U.S.A.! Hit the open road! Sound like a travel brochure? Well, traveling around our country is big business and a popular pastime for many people. Listed here, in order of popularity, are the states and theme parks that we most like to visit. How many have you been to?

California	New York	New Jersey
Florida	Illinois	Georgia
Texas	Nevada	Virginia
	Pennsylvania	

Most Popular U.S. Theme Parks

PARK	LOCATION
Magic Kingdom, Walt Disney World	Lake Buena Vista, Florida
Disneyland	Anaheim, California
Epcot, Walt Disney World	Lake Buena Vista, Florida
Disney-MGM Studios, Walt Disney World	Lake Buena Vista, Florida
Disney's Animal Kingdom, Walt Disney World	Lake Buena Vista, Florida
Universal Studios Florida	Orlando, Florida
Disney's California Adventure	Anaheim, California
Universal's Islands of Adventure	Orlando, Florida
SeaWorld Orlando	Orlando, Florida
Universal Studios Hollywood	Los Angeles, California

 More people visit California than any other state. But can you name the least visited state? Hint: Its town of Rugby is the geographic center of North America. That's right — beautiful North Dakota!

Are We There Yet?

Millions of tourists visit the United States each year, with the highest number coming from Canada, Mexico, Great Britain, Japan, and Germany. Where do they go? Here are the top destinations of tourists from outside the United States. How many of these states and cities have you visited?

Most Popular States to Visit

New York • Florida • California • Hawaii • Nevada • Illinois • Massachusetts • Texas • New Jersey • Pennsylvania

Most Popular Cities to Visit

New York, New York • Los Angeles, California • Miami, Florida • Orlando, Florida • Oahu/Honolulu, Hawaii • San Francisco, California • Las Vegas, Nevada • Washington, D.C. • Chicago, Illinois • Boston, Massachusetts

Craters on Earth

Just like the moon, the Earth's surface has been struck by asteroids and comets over the centuries. You can easily see these craters on the moon (the biggest ones form the dark features that we call the Man in the Moon). But on Earth many of the craters are covered by vegetation or are deep under the sea. Some have filled up with water and are now lakes. More than 160 such craters have been documented; here is a list of the 15 biggest. How big is big? The Vredefort crater would almost completely cover the state of Colorado!

CRATER	DIAMETER (MI./KM)	LOCATION
Vredefort	186.4/300	South Africa
Sudbury	155.3/250	Canada
Chicxulub	105.6/170	Mexico
Manicouagan	62.1/100	Canada
Popigai	62.1/100	Russia
Acraman	55.9/90	Australia
Chesapeake Bay	55.9/90	United States
Puchezh-Katunki	49.7/80	Russia
Morokweng	43.5/70	South Africa
Kara	40.4/65	Russia
Beaverhead	37.3/60	United States
Tookoonooka	34.2/55	Australia
Charlevoix	33.6/54	Canada
Kara-Kul	32.3/52	Tajikistan
Siljan	32.3/52	Sweden

ACTIVE
Volcanoes

They only make the news when they blow their tops, but these volcanoes are always active. They can be found all over our planet. The volcanoes on this list have displayed recent activity, whether that's venting steam or smoke, or actually spewing hot lava.

VOLCANO	LOCATION	VOLCANO	LOCATION
Arenal	Costa Rica	Kilauea	Hawaii
Asama	Japan	Manam	Papua New Guinea
Aso	Japan	Mayon	Philippines
Awu	Indonesia	Mount St. Helens	United States
Bagana	Papua New Guinea	Nyamuragira	Congo
Bezymianny	Russia	Nyiragongo	Congo
Colima	Mexico	Ol Doinyo Lengai	Tanzania
Concepción	Nicaragua	Rabaul	Papua New Guinea
Dukono	Indonesia	Sakura-jima	Japan
Erebus	Antarctica	San Cristobal	Ecuador
Erta Ale	Ethiopia	Sangay	Ecuador
Etna	Italy	Semeru	Indonesia
Fuego	Guatemala	Shishaldin	United States
Glaeras	Colombia	Shiveluch	Russia
Grimsvötn	Iceland	Soputan	Indonesia
Karangetang	Indonesia	Stromboli	Italy
Karymsky	Russia	Tungurahua	Ecuador
Kerinci	Indonesia	Veniaminof	United States

Coral Reefs

Warm, shallow water and sunlight provide a great environment for coral reefs. A coral reef consists of tiny animals that deposit calcium on the sea floor. When the animals die, their exoskeletons (yes, their skeleton is on the outside of their body! Must be fun at Halloween!) pile up to form the basis for the reef. The reef then becomes a home for more living coral, plants, fish, and other marine life.

Types of Reefs

Atoll reef   Continuous barrier reef around a lagoon

Barrier reef   Reef that is separated from the shore by a lagoon

Fringing reef   Reef platforms that extend out from the shoreline

The World's Three Biggest Reefs

1. **Great Barrier Reef**   Queensland, Australia
2. **Barrier Reef of Belize**   Belize, Central America
3. **Indonesian Coral Reefs**   Around Indonesia

Reef Brief

• A temperature of 65°F (18°C) and higher in the winter is needed to support a coral reef, so coral reefs are found in the tropical and subtropical regions of the world's oceans.

• The Great Barrier Reef is the world's largest protected marine area. It is home to more than 4,000 species of mollusks, 1,500 species of fish, 215 bird species, and 16 different types of sea snake.

• If the Great Barrier Reef ran across the American mainland, it would stretch from Los Angeles almost all the way to Chicago! (Of course, if it did, it wouldn't be as wet.)

HIGHEST
Waterfalls

You could take a high dive over these highest waterfalls, but it would be a very long way to the bottom! In comparison to these mighty cataracts (a fancy name for a waterfall), Niagara Falls (on the border between Canada and New York State) is only 176 feet (53.6 m) high.

WATERFALL	LOCATION	HEIGHT (FT.)	(M)
Angel	Venezuela	3,281	1,000
Tugela	South Africa	3,000	914
Utigord	Norway	2,625	800
Monge	Norway	2,540	774
Mutarazi	Zimbabwe	2,499	762
Yosemite	United States	2,425	739
Pieman	Australia	2,346	715
Espelands	Norway	2,307	703
Lower Mar Valley	Norway	2,151	655
Tyssestrengene	Norway	2,123	647
Cuquenan	Venezuela	2,000	610
Sentinel	United States	2,000	610
Dudhsagar	India	1,969	600
Sutherland	New Zealand	1,904	580
Kjell	Norway	1,841	561

How did Angel Falls get its name? American pilot Jimmy Angel flew his airplane near the falls in 1933 while looking for a place to start a mine. He returned later to land atop the mountain from which the falls, well . . . fall. His plane got stuck and it took him 11 days to climb down!

How Dry Are We?

The award for the driest place in the world goes to the Atacama Desert in Chile. That area averages about 0.004 inches (0.01 cm) of rain per year. Some areas of that desert haven't had rain in recorded history. Yet some people do live there. Scientists study the Atacama Desert to find out what kinds of organisms (other than people, who can buy water if they need it) can live in these ultra-dry conditions. Here are the world's driest places.

PLACE	AVERAGE ANNUAL RAINFALL	
	IN.	CM
Atacama, Chile	0.004	0.01
Arica, Chile	0.012	0.03
Al'Kufrah, Libya	0.012	0.03
Aswan, Egypt	0.012	0.03
Luxor, Egypt	0.012	0.03
Ica, Peru	0.035	0.09
Wadi Halfa, Sudan	0.039	0.10
Iquique, Chile	0.079	0.20
Pelican Point, Namibia	0.126	0.32
Aoelef, Algeria	0.189	0.48
Callao, Peru	0.189	0.48

Tropical Rain Forests

Tropical rain forests are located within the Earth's tropic zones, which are near the Equator all around the globe. The Tropics of Cancer and Capricorn (see page 89) mark the borders of this area. Only six percent of the world's land is rain forest. The Amazon rain forest in South America is the largest, and also has the widest diversity of plants and animals. Here are some other facts about these important ecosystems.

● Tropical rain forests receive anywhere from 60 inches (152 cm) to 400 inches (1,026 cm) of rain each year. Average temperatures range from 70° F to 90° F (21° to 50° C).

● Tropical rain forests can be found on the continents of Africa, Asia, and South America.

PERCENT OF THE WORLD'S TROPICAL RAIN FORESTS

Africa, Madagascar	19%
Asia, Pacific Islands, Australia	25%
Central and South America	56%

● Tropical rain forests can be categorized by their wet and dry seasons.

Flooded forests	rain throughout the year, flooded throughout the year
Seasonally dry forests	dry and wet seasons
Seasonally flooded forests	rain throughout the year with some months of flooding

● Tropical rain forests have four layers.

Forest floor	floor of the forest with some plants, receives little direct sunlight
Understory	small trees and plants that grow under the canopy
Canopy	tops of the trees that form a canopy-like cover over the whole forest
Emergent	topmost layer, trees that tower above the rest of the forest

● Countries with the most tropical rain forest area.

Brazil	1,125,857 sq. mi. (2,915,956 sq. km)
Indonesia	362,267 sq. mi. (938,267 sq. km)
Dem. Rep. of Congo	233,348 sq. mi. (604,369 sq. km)

Spelunking, Anyone?

Do you want to explore unknown lands, deep and mysterious? Try exploring caves! The sport is called caving, potholing, or spelunking, and the adventurers who love it often find new caves or deeper passages in existing caves. That means this listing of deepest caves can change rapidly. Here's something to think about: A mile is 5,280 feet (1,609 meters), so many of these caves descend more than a mile below the surface!

CAVE/COUNTRY	DEPTH (FT.)	(M)
Voronja Cave/Abkhazia*	7,021	2,140
Lamprechtsofen/Austria	5,354	1,632
Gouffre Mirolda/France	5,335	1,626
Reseau Jean Bernard/France	5,256	1,602
Torca del Cerro del Cueveon/Spain	5,213	1,589
Sarma/Abkhazia*	5,062	1,543
Cehi 2/Slovenia	5,030	1,533
Shakta Vjacheslav Pantjuknina/Abkhazia*	4,948	1,508
Sistema Cheve/Mexico	4,869	1,484
Sistema Huautla/Mexico	4,839	1,475

*An autonomous republic within the country of Georgia

Which of these words is not used by cavers to describe some sort of cave feature? *Chimney, drapery, gork, grike, hall, meander, passage, pillar, pipe, tunnel.* The answer? All those terms describe features of a cave except *gork*.

AROUND
The World

Many people have made the long trip around the world — some faster than others. The first to circle the globe were aboard the British ship *Victoria*, which took three years to make the trip in 1522. Since then, people have circumnavigated the world (gone all the way around) in just about every sort of vehicle you can think of. Here's a list of some of the most important or record-setting trips. And although the world's been around for quite a while, you can see from this list that people are still finding newer and faster ways to get around it.

TRAVELERS	TRAVELED BY	DATES	TIME
Hugo Eckener	Graf Zeppelin airship	1929	21 days
USS Triton	submarine (without surfacing)	1960	61 days
Dave Kunst	foot	1970–1974	1,573 days
Saloo and Neena Choudhury	car	1989	70 days
Kay Cottee	boat (nonstop)	1987–1988	189 days
Steve Fossett	gas balloon	2002	14 days
Chris and Erin Ratay	motorcycles	1999–2003	4 years
Alastair Humphreys	bicycle	2001–2005	1,555 days
Michael and Sandy Groves	SUV	2003–2005	815 days
Steve Fossett	jet (without refueling)	2005	67 hours
Bruno Peyron and crew	sailboat	2005	51 days

21 Pairs of Shoes

Dave Kunst left his hometown of Waseca, Minnesota, in June 1970. He didn't get back home for more than four years! Where was he? Well, literally, all around the world. It took Dave that long to walk completely around the globe. His mega-power-walk ended up covering 14,450 miles (23,255 km). Along the way, the foot-weary traveler (hasn't he heard of airplanes?!) wore out 21 hard-working pairs of shoes!

PLACES NAMED FOR
Food

Bet you didn't think you'd get hungry while reading about geography, did you? Here's a list of places in the United States that are named for food. You could gather all of these places together and put them on Dinner Island, found in Washington. Be sure to bring your utensils, found in Fork, Maryland. The most popular food name is Orange, found as a city or county name in at least 11 states. Enjoy reading — and eating.

LOCATION	STATE	LOCATION	STATE
Almond	WI	Nectar	AL
Bacon	MO	Olive	IL, KA, NY, OH
Beans	NH	Orange	CA, IL, IN, KA, MN, ND, NJ, NY, OH, PA, WI
Berry	AL, KY		
Blackberry	IL	Pancake	PA
Blueberry	MN	Pineapple	AL
Cherry	KA	Plum	KA, PA
Cranberry	OH, PA	Rice	MN
Cocoa	FL	Rye	NH, NY
Fries	VA	Salmon	ID
Greens	NH	Sandwich	NH
Lamb	IN	Strawberry	KA
Mead	CO	Sugar Loaf	PA
Mulberry	FL	Walnut	CA, IA, IL, IN, KA, MS, OH

Tasty Places

Over there on page 100 are places named for food; here's a page where we return the favor. A number of well-known foods are named after places. However, sometimes the geographic reference will throw you a curve. For example, Philadelphia cream cheese was invented in Chester, New York. Enjoy a tour of the world with these globetrotting foods.

PLACE	FOOD
Alaska	Baked Alaska
Boston, Mass.	Boston baked beans
Boston, Mass.	Boston cream pie
Brazil	Brazil nut
Brussels, Belgium	Brussels sprouts
Cayenne, French Guyana	Cayenne pepper
Cheddar, England	Cheddar cheese
Frankfurt am Main, Germany	Frankfurters
Hamburg, Germany	Hamburger
New York City	Manhattan clam chowder
Beijing, China	Peking duck
Switzerland	Swiss cheese
Tabasco, Mexico	Tabasco sauce
Worcester, England	Worcestershire sauce
Yorkshire, England	Yorkshire pudding

Learn to Love Them

Okay, we all know that nobody likes Brussels sprouts. Well, almost nobody. In case you won't eat them, however, here are some facts to chew on: They are a form of cabbage. They were first described in 1587. Long Island, New York, is America's Brussels-sprouts-growing center.

See . . . Shells

You know that tongue twister "She sells seashells by the seashore"? Before you (or she) sell any seashells, you have to find them! The shells that we gather come from mollusks and are the exoskeletons of the animals. The two main types of mollusk shells people collect are univalves (the shell is all in one part, like a snail) and bivalves (the shell comes in two parts, like a clam). Here are some popular examples of each type.

Univalves
Abalone
Bubble shells
Common sundials
Conchs
Cone shells
Cowries
Dove shells
Helmet shells
Limpets
Marginellas
Moon shells
Murexes
Nerites
Periwinkles
Slipper shells
Snails
Star shells
Top shells
Tritons
Turban shells
Turrids
Whelks
Wentletraps
Volutes
Worm shells

Bivalves
Ark shells
Bittersweets
Clams
Cockles
False angel wings
Jewel boxes
Jingle shells
Kitten's paws
Lucines
Mussels
Oysters
Pen shells
Scallops
Shipworms

Sandcastle
Secrets

Whether you're a king, or a princess, or your name is just Duke, you can own a castle — as long as it's made of sand! Sandcastles can be built in your backyard sandbox or next to the water's edge. From simple mounds to elaborately carved walls and turrets, your castle can be as amazing as your creativity (and patience) allow. Here are some tips from experts on what you need for a simple castle.

The Basics

Sand: Wet sand near the water's edge works best.

Water: Add water as the sand dries out.

Bucket: How else can you carry the sand and water?

Shovel: It's useful for the major digging.

Other tools

Table utensils: Knives, forks, and spoons for smoothing and decorating.

Spray bottle: Filled with water, to keep the sand moist.

Plastic food containers: To mold various shapes for the castle.

Other tools for molding sand: These can include a melon baller, measuring cups, pastry knife, meat mallet, paint scrapers, trowels, putty knives, and paintbrushes.

Tips

▲ Pick a spot away from incoming waves.

▲ Start with a big pile of sand and work from the top down, sculpting as you go.

▲ For stairs, form a ramp first and then cut the stairs in.

▲ A paintbrush is useful for brushing away excess sand.

▲ Spray lightly with water as you finish each section to hold it firm.

▲ Want to go really big? The pros sometimes use wooden forms to create big shapes!

World & Weather
Game Page

This is a book of lists, of course, but sometimes things end up on the wrong list. In this game, read over these mini-lists of words and terms from this chapter. One of the terms doesn't belong; just find the item that's in the wrong list. Then, fill in a word that briefly describes what the list is about (minus the "wrong" one, of course). For example, which of "rain, snow, sheep, and sleet" doesn't belong? Sheep, right? But that's an easy one. Good luck!

1. Foraker, Whitney, Rainier, Washington, Vancouver: _____

2. Yong, Moses, Loretan, Martini, Carsolla: _____

3. Palau, Monaco, Vatican, Malta, Seychelles: _____

4. Sacramento, Bakersfield, New Orleans, New York, Charlotte: _____

5. Florida, Illinois, Alaska, Hawaii, New Jersey, New York: _____

6. Manam, Mayon, Miami, Asama, Awu, Aso: _____

7. Al-Aqsa, Aoelef, Arica, Atacama, Aswan: _____

8. Kunst, Fossett, Gordon, Peyron, Cottee: _____

9. Salmon, Almond, Peanut, Lamb, Walnut: _____

10. Whelks, Tritons, Conchs, Volutes, Corks: _____

CHAPTER FOUR

Science

Chemistry, botany, dinosaurs — rah!
Stinky plants, yucky skin, passing gas — ha!
C'mon, who says science is boring?
This chapter proves 'em all wrong!

GREAT
Galaxy Names

We are not alone. Astronomers have identified more than 500,000 galaxies in addition to our home galaxy, the Milky Way. The galaxies closest to us, plus any that are studied often, usually get names. Some of those star-studded names are listed below.

Just a lucky few get names, though. Because there are so many galaxies, there just aren't enough names to go around. So all the galaxies also get numbers. For example, the Lost Galaxy (which obviously has been found, or else it wouldn't have a name!) is NGC 4535 (NGC stands for New General Catalog, an international listing of heavenly bodies).

Andromeda	Hercules A	Seashell
Aquarius Dwarf	Hydra A	Shapley-Ames
Bears Paw	Leo I	Siamese Twins
Black Eye	Mice	Silver Coin
Cartwheel	Pancake	Sombrero
Draco Dwarf	Papillion	Sunflower
The Garland	Pinwheel	Whirlpool
Helix	Pisces Cloud	Wild's Galaxy

Galaxy Guide

There are four basic galaxy shapes:

Barred Spiral	Central bar with an arm at each end
Elliptical	Circular to oval, no arms
Irregular	Clouds of stars, no defined shape
Spiral	Arms of stars curve out from a center

What's in Here?

If you split the Earth in half (in your imagination, please!), or just cut out a wedge like a piece of cake, you would see the layers of matter that make up the Earth. We spend our lives on the top layer, which is called the crust. Below that are miles and miles of other stuff, both squishy and solid. For instance, if you really wanted to dig a hole to China, you'd have to tunnel through hot molten rock. Have fun!

LAYER	WHERE IT IS	WHAT IT IS
Atmosphere	Surrounds the Earth	Air
Crust	Surface of the Earth	Layer of soil and rock
Mantle	Under the crust	Layer of hot, molten rock
Outer core	Center of the Earth	Layer of hot, molten rock
Inner core	Center of the Earth	Solid rock

LAYERS OF THE OCEANS

Photic/Topmost layer

Bathyl/Middle layer

Abyssal/Bottom layer

How deep into the Earth have human beings gone? That honor goes to a group of cavers who have explored the deepest cave on Earth. The Krubera Cave in the central Asian nation of Abkhazia has been mapped as far as 6,824 ft. (2,080 m) below the surface. But even that is only a tiny fraction of the distance (3,963 miles/6.378 km) to the center of the Earth.

Phases of the Moon

The moon is the same size and shape all the time, but from our position on Earth it seems to change shape as it orbits the Earth every 29 days. These apparent changes are called phases, and are caused by the Earth blocking light from the sun so it can't shine on the moon. At different parts of the moon's orbit, different areas of its surface are blocked. It's all an illusion, but we have names for each phase, anyway.

New
Dark circle, little visible illumination

Waxing crescent
Sliver of illumination on the right side

First quarter
Half the moon is illuminated on the right side

Waxing gibbous
Three fourths of the moon is illuminated from the right side

Full
Whole moon is illuminated

Waning gibbous
Three fourths of the moon is illuminated from the left side

Last quarter
Half the moon is illuminated on the left side

Waning crescent
Sliver of illumination on the left side

Who's in the Moon?

Have you ever seen the Man in the Moon? What about Grand MaMoon? Over the years, many people have looked up at the moon and seen, in the dark and light patches of its surface, a man's or woman's face. Look up at a full moon and use your imagination to find these figures in the moon, from tales told by various cultures around the world. And remember, despite the holes, the moon is not made of cheese.

The Lady in the Moon

○ A Chinese story tells of Chang Er, who drank the elixir of life and flew to the moon.

○ In Mayan mythology, Ix Chel, the Lady Rainbow, is the moon goddess.

○ In Roman mythology, Diana is the goddess of the moon.

○ In Greek mythology, Artemis is the goddess of the moon.

○ In Maori legend, Rona is the woman in the moon, and she carries a bucket of water.

The Man in the Moon

○ A Chinese story tells of Wu Kang, banished to the moon because he was impatient with his life.

○ An Australian Aborigine legend says the man in the moon is a creature named Bunyip, who climbed a tree and stared at everything with one eye. That eye became the moon.

○ In Aztec mythology, Huitzilopochtli cut off Coyolxauhqui's head. He threw it into the sky and it became the moon.

○ In Hindu mythology, the moon god, Soma, travels across the sky in a chariot pulled by white horses.

○ In Japanese legend, Tsuki-Yomi, the moon god, lives on the moon.

The Rabbit in the Moon

○ In this Chinese tale, because the rabbit offered his body as food for the wise sages, he was allowed to live in the Moon Palace and was called the Jade Rabbit.

Space Shuttle
Trips

The space shuttle has provided us with a way to travel back and forth to space from Earth. The official name of the space shuttle program is Space Transportation System, or STS for short, because the main job of the shuttle is to carry stuff — it's like a big space truck. The shuttles have carried payloads (cargo) and astronauts to the International Space Station, launched equipment farther into space, and even taken astronauts to fix the stuff that's already up there. More than 115 space shuttle missions have been launched. Here's a complete list of how many missions each shuttle has flown.

SHUTTLE NAME	FIRST LAUNCHED	NO. OF FLIGHTS
*Columbia**	April 12, 1981	28
*Challenger***	April 4, 1983	10
Discovery	August 30, 1984	32
Atlantis	October 3, 1985	27
Endeavor	May 7, 1992	19

*In 2003, *Columbia* broke up during re-entry, killing all seven of its crew.

**Challenger* exploded during liftoff in 1986; all seven astronauts died.

Shuttle Stuff

The space shuttle provides endless lists of stuff. From the list of animals who have flown in it to the list of food the astronauts eat up there (see page 235), life on the space shuttle is one big checklist. Here's a list of interesting facts about the space shuttle with which to amaze your friends and impress your teachers.

The *Endeavor* space shuttle cost $2.1 billon to build.

The shuttle is 184 feet (56.08 m) long.

The orbiter has a wingspan of 78 feet (24 m).

The shuttle weighs 4.5 million pounds (2.04 million kg); that's about equal to 150 school buses!

The maximum payload (how much it can carry) is 59,000 pounds (26,786 kg); that's as much as the weight of two school buses.

Countdown for a shuttle launch actually begins three days before the launch.

Landing delays have been caused by cloud cover, rain, high wind, fog, and low visibility.

In 1995, yellow flicker woodpeckers (yes . . . birds!) pecked 195 holes in the external tank foam of *Discovery*, causing a launch delay.

The shuttle reaches altitudes of between 200 and 385 miles (322 and 620 km) while orbiting the Earth.

The longest mission was *Columbia* in 1996; it lasted 17 days, 53 minutes, 18 seconds.

Junk in Space

Human beings have been shooting stuff into space since the 1950s. A lot of it is still up there! There are now more than 9,000 objects larger than a baseball floating around as "space junk." Even a postage-stamp-size paint chip can cause great damage to a spacecraft, so all that stuff can be dangerous. (The space shuttles have needed more than 80 window replacements because of damage caused by space junk hitting them at top speeds of 22,000 mph/35,000 kph.) Some stuff has fallen toward Earth; most of that burns up on the way in, but some of it plunks down on the ground. Here's a list of some of the things that are still up there, whizzing above our heads.

50 Delta rocket upper stages
Blown-off hatches
Insulation

Lost glove
Main fuel tank
Metal mesh
Non-working satellites
Paint chips
Pressurization sphere
Trash bags
Nuts and bolts
Skylab chunks
Solar cells
Solid fuel fragments
Space probes
Titanium sphere
Working satellites*

(*We know where all of those are!)

More Than Just Tang®

Many products we take for granted did not exist before the space program invented them, or developed the materials or the technology used to make them. Scientists had specific needs for space travel and they developed products to answer these needs. These inventions first used in the space program now benefit us in our everyday lives. By the way, Tang was a powdered orange drink later sold to the public as the "stuff that the astronauts drink."

Bar coding

Dust buster

Ear thermometer

Emergency response robot

Enriched baby food

Fire-resistant fabric

Flat-panel TV

Fogless goggles

Freeze-dried food

Hang gliders

Home security system

Joystick controller

Magnetic liquids

Medical imaging

Portable power tools

Satellite TV

Scratch-resistant lenses

Self-righting life raft

Smoke detector

Tap water purifier

Trash compactor

Virtual reality

Voice-controlled wheelchair

Chemistry Basics

Do you like experimenting with liquids that change colors or make a big stink? Congratulations — you like chemistry! Chemistry is the science of how stuff (also known as matter) combines with other stuff. Here is a list of some of the basic terms you'll see in chemistry.

Atom
The smallest part of an element that still has all the properties of the element.

Capillary action
When liquid rises through a small tube or opening.

Chemical reaction
When substances combine and change.

Compound
Two or more elements joined together to form a new substance.

Dispersion
When the particles of a substance scatter throughout another substance.

Dissolve
Adding solids or gases to liquids so that they disappear in the liquid.

Element
A substance made of the same kinds of atoms, which cannot be broken down.

Gas
A substance that does not have a definite shape or volume, but tends to keep expanding.

Liquid
A substance that has definite volume but no definite shape.

Matter
Anything that has volume and mass (size and weight). It comes in three states: solid, liquid, and gas.

Melting point
The temperature at which a solid changes and melts into a liquid.

Molecule
A group of two or more atoms that are joined together.

Neutron
A subatomic particle within the nucleus of the atom; it has no electrical charge.

Periodic table
A list of all the elements, by their atomic number (the number of protons found in the nucleus).

Proton
A subatomic particle within the nucleus of the atom; it has a positive charge.

Sediment
The material that settles at the bottom of a liquid.

Solid
A substance that has a definite size and shape.

Solution
A liquid mixture with atoms of one substance spread evenly in another substance.

Making It Metric

While we in the United States measure everything in feet and inches, ounces and pounds, the rest of the world went metric long ago. The metric system is also used by scientists worldwide, so even in the United States, we all need to know it. Confused about how to convert back and forth? We have just what you need:

Need to change temperature?

From Fahrenheit to Centigrade (Celsius): Subtract 32 from the F temperature, multiply the difference by 5, and divide the answer by 9.

From Centigrade (Celsius) to Fahrenheit: Multiply the C temperature by 9, divide the result by 5, then add 32.

Need to change volume measurements?

1 teaspoon = 5 milliliters

1 tablespoon = 15 milliliters

1 fluid ounce = 30 milliliters

1 cup = 237 milliliters

1 pint = 473 milliliters

1 quart = 0.95 liter

1.06 quarts = 1 liter

1 gallon = 3.8 liters

Need to change weight measurements?

1 ounce = 28 grams

3.5 ounces = 100 grams

1 pound = 454 grams

2.20 pounds = 1 kilogram

1 ton = 2,000 pounds = 907 kilograms

Need to change length, width, or distance measurements?

0.0001 inch = 1 millimeter

1 inch = 25 millimeters

1 foot = 30.5 centimeters

1 yard = 914 centimeters

1 fathom = 1.829 meters

1 mile = 1.609 kilometers

Need to change area measurements?

1 square inch = 6.5 square centimeters

1 square foot = 929 square centimeters

1 square yard = 0.836 square meters

1 acre = 0.405 hectare

1 square mile = 259 square hectares

Uni-, Bi-, Tri-, and Beyond

Science involves a lot of counting. You'll run across all sorts of prefixes that describe "how many." (A prefix is a syllable that comes before the main part of the word.) For example, poly means "many" in Greek, and we use it in a lot of English words, such as *polygon* (a shape with many sides), *polydactyl* (having more than the normal number of fingers or toes), and *polyglot* (knowing many languages). Some of these prefixes tell you exactly how many. Check out this list of "how many" prefixes, along with what language they originally came from.

PREFIX	MEANING/ ORIGINAL LANGUAGE	PREFIX	MEANING/ ORIGINAL LANGUAGE
Mono	1/Greek	Oct	8/Latin
Uni	1/Latin	Ennea	9/Greek
Bi	2/Latin	Non	9/Latin
Di	2/Greek	De	10/Latin
Duo	2/Latin	Deca	10/Greek
Tri	3/Latin	Hendeca	11/Greek
Quad	4/Latin	Unde	11/Latin
Quart	4/Latin	Duodec	12/Latin
Tetra	4/Greek	Dodeca	12/Greek
Penta	5/Greek	Centi	100/Latin
Quint	5/Latin	Hecto	100/Greek
Hexa	6/Greek	Milli	1,000/Latin
Sex	6/Latin	Kilo	1,000/Greek
Sept	7/Latin	Mega	1 million/Greek
Hepta	7/Greek	Giga	1 billion/Latin
		Tera	1 trillion/Greek

Power Up!

Need to find the square, cube, or higher power of a number? You can do the multiplication yourself (a lot of work) or use this handy chart (no work at all!) to find your answer.

NUMBER	POWER 2ND	3RD	4TH	5TH	6TH	7TH
2	4	8	16	32	64	128
3	9	27	81	243	729	2,187
4	16	64	256	1,024	4,096	16,384
5	25	125	625	3,125	15,625	78,125
6	36	216	1,296	7,776	46,656	279,936
7	49	343	2,401	16,807	117,649	823,543
8	64	512	4,096	32,768	262,144	2,097,152
9	81	729	6,561	59,049	531,441	4,782,969
10	100	1,000	10,000	100,000	1,000,000	10,000,000
11	121	1,331	14,641	161,051	1,771,561	19,487,171
12	144	1,728	20,736	248,832	2,985,984	35,831,808

Plant Medicine

Many common plants found in homes and gardens can be used for healing. Their uses come down through folklore and experience. Some of these plants are eaten; others are put on the skin. Be careful what you try and eat! These medicines should only be made by someone who knows what they are doing. This list of plants shows the conditions they treat.

Aloe	wounds, burns, sunburn
Anise	coughs
Apples	constipation, high cholesterol
Cabbage	poor digestion, achy joints, skin problems, fever
Cinnamon	colds, arthritis, rheumatism
Eucalyptus	infected wounds, bacterial infections
Garlic	high cholesterol, weak immune system
Ginger	upset stomach, travel sickness, nausea
Ginseng	low energy
Green tea	low energy, digestive problems
Honeysuckle	asthma
Lavender	sleep problems
Licorice	upset stomach
Oats	high cholesterol
Peony	nervous conditions
Peppermint	indigestion
Plantain	constipation
Primrose	headaches, colds
Rhubarb	constipation
Skullcap	nervous disorders, headaches

Tallest Trees

They come in all sorts of sizes but (mostly) in one shape: straight up and down. Trees provide us with air to breathe, fruit to eat, and wood to sit on and live in. Some trees can be real skyscrapers. Here's a list of amazing facts about the world's tallest trees.

Tallest Trees Ever

Loggers in Australia cut down a eucalyptus tree that was 435 feet (132.6 m) in 1872. A coast redwood that measured 372 feet (113.4 m) fell in 1991 in California.

Tallest Living Tree

The Stratosphere Giant, another coast redwood, stands proudly in a secret location (to keep it from being swamped by tourists) in Humboldt Redwoods Park in northern California. It towers 370 feet (112.7 m). However, in September 2006, scientists found three nearby trees that topped it; if confirmed, the new tallest tree would be a 378-foot (115.2-m) redwood known as Hyperion.

Tallest Species

Coast redwoods, Australian eucalyptus, Australian flowering mountain ash all can top 330 feet (100 m).

How Tall Can They Go?

An article in the British journal *Science* reported that the tallest a tree could be is 426 feet (130 m). Why a limit? Because the taller a tree is, the harder it is for it to get water and food all the way to the top. Rain helps, but trees live mostly on what's inside them, and that's a long elevator ride to the top branches!

MEDICAL Machines

From machines that measure your heartbeat to robots that perform surgery, no hospital or doctor's office is complete without dozens of machines. Here's a list of some of the more common ones and what they do.

CAT No, not a feline, but a machine that produces a kind of internal picture of a person's body. It stands for Computed Axial Tomography, and delivers an almost 3-D vision of what's going on inside you.

Defibrillator This is the one they use when they yell "Clear!" Two paddles are placed on a person whose heart has stopped. Using electric current from this machine, doctors try to restart the heart.

Dialysis machine When a person's kidneys aren't working, this machine cleans his or her blood. Dialysis machines are like washing machines for blood.

EEG This electroencephelogram measures brain waves.

EKG (or ECG) Using wires attached to a person, the electrocardiogram measures all sorts of information about how the heart is beating. It spits out a graph on a narrow paper strip that a doctor can read.

Pulse oximeter Hooked up to a patient's finger or ear, this machine measures how much oxygen is in the blood.

Ultrasound Another way that doctors look inside us is with this machine. Sound waves bounce in and out and the machine produces a black-and-white still or moving picture.

Types of Doctors

Many doctors practice a special branch of medicine. Depending on your needs and symptoms, you may visit one or more of these specialists someday.

Allergist	immune system, allergies
General Practitioner	general, overall health
Anesthesiologist	uses anesthesia to relieve pain
Cardiologist	circulatory system, heart
Dermatologist	skin
Emergency Physician	emergency treatment
Gastroenterologist	digestive system
Gynecologist	female reproductive system
Hematologist	circulatory system, blood
Neurologist	nervous system
Pathologist	body tissues, secretions, fluids
Pediatrician	babies, kids
Psychiatrist	mental and emotional disorders
Obstetrician	pregnancy
Ophthalmologist	eyes, vision
Oncologist	cancer
Podiatrist	feet
Radiologist	X-rays
Urologist	urinary system

Skin Deep

What's the largest organ of your body? Would you guess the stomach or intestines? Not even close! It's your skin. If you stretched it all out, the skin on an adult covers an area about the size of a shower curtain. Your great big skin is actually made up of three layers. The top layer, the epidermis, is the part you see. It actually renews itself about every 40 days. Below that are other layers that each have a job to do. Here's what's in your skin, from the outside, in.

Epidermis (5 layers)
Stratum corneum
Stratum licidum
Granular layer
Spiny layer
Basal layer

Dermis (2 layers)
Papillary
Reticular

The dermis contains: blood vessels, hair roots, nerves, sweat glands, lymph vessels

Subcutaneous fat (1 layer)

The subcutaneous fat layer contains: adipose fat cells, larger blood vessels, nerves

? Hey, your epidermis is showing! (Love that joke.) To protect your epidermis from too much sun, use sunscreen as protection against skin cancer. The Skin Cancer Foundation suggests products with an SPF (Sun Protection Factor) of at least 15.

Open Wide!
Types of Teeth

Your first set of teeth, known as the baby or milk teeth, number 20, but the magic number is 32. When all of your adult teeth finally push through your gums, you will have 32 teeth. Human teeth come in these specific categories.

Each jaw has:

4 incisors   x 2 jaws = **8** incisors

2 canine or eye teeth or cuspids x 2 jaws = **4** canine teeth

4 premolars or bicuspids   x 2 jaws = **8** premolars

6 molars   x 2 jaws = **12** molars

(Your wisdom teeth are the end molars on each side of your upper and lower jaws — you have 4.)

Don't Go to the Dentist — *Be* the Dentist!

Lots of kids grow up wanting to be doctors. But maybe some of you should think about being dentists, too. There are about 160,000 working dentists in the United States, but enrollment at dental schools is only going up a tiny bit each year, and since everyone has teeth, it's a pretty steady job. Plus, the average salary is more than $170,000 a year. There's gold in them thar teeth (for you and for the patient!).

Big Body Parts

Think you've got big feet? Take a look at these folks! At the moment these people claim the titles for big body parts, according to Guinness World Records®.

Tallest

Man	Robert Pershing Wadlow, USA	8 ft. 11.1 in./2.72 m
Woman	Zeng Jinlian, China	8 ft. 1.75 in./2.48 m
Living man	Xi Shun, China	7 ft. 8.95 in./2.35 m
Living woman	Sandy Allen, USA	7 ft. 7.25 in./2.31 m
NBA player	Gheorghe Muresan, Romania	7 ft. 7 in./2.31 m

Largest/Longest

Arm hair	David Hruska, USA	3.18 in./9.7 cm
Ear hair	Radhakant Bajpai, India	5.19 in./13.2 cm
Fingernails	Lee Redmond, USA	295.8 in./7.51 m
Hair	Xie Qiuping, China	221.54 in./5.63 m
Hands	Robert Pershing Wadlow, USA	12.75 in./32.3 cm
Kidney stone	Peter Baulman, Australia	12.5 oz./356 g
Leg hair	Tim Stinton, Australia	4.88 in./12.4 cm
Neck	Padaung Tribal Women, Myanmar	15.75 in./40 cm
Nose (living man)	Mehmet Ozyurek, Turkey	3.46 in./8.8 cm
Tongue	Stephen Taylor, Britain	3.7 in./9.4 cm

Heaviest

Twins	Billy Leon McCrary, USA	743 lbs./337 kg
	Benny Lloyd McCrary, USA	723 lbs./328 kg
Living athlete	Emanuel Yarbrough, USA	770 lbs./349 kg
Sumo wrestler	Chad Rowan (Akebono), USA*	501 lbs./349 kg
Man	Jon Brower Minnoch, USA	1,400 lbs./635 kg
Woman	Rosalie Bradford, USA	1,200 lbs./544 kg

*He's now a Japanese citizen.

Thanks, Sun!

Energy from the sun powers everything on Earth. What's that, you say? Gas powers cars? Well, what do you think helped grow the plants that fed the dinosaurs, who would become oil and gas millions of years later? Solar power is becoming more and more a regular part of people's energy supply. Here are some facts about solar power to impress your friends with. Please wear sunscreen and don't look at the facts directly.

✳ In just one hour, the Earth is hit with more solar power than it uses in a year!

✳ Japan produces half of the world's solar "cells," the devices that gather in the sun's rays and help convert it to electricity.

✳ Solar cells covering 0.3 percent of the United States could provide all of the country's electricity needs.

✳ In some cases, your house's solar cells could produce more electricity than you need. You could then "cell" (ha-ha, get it?) the extra electricity back to the power company; your house could make money!

✳ One of the most popular ways to use solar energy is to heat water. Pipes inside the solar cells heat the water, which is then distributed to the house.

✳ Solar-powered cars? Well, not in your garage yet, but maybe someday. College students and scientists take part in annual competitions to create and race solar-powered cars, some of which can go at highway speeds for hundreds of miles.

Passing Gas

Gas — the kind cars run on — is expensive, and the world's supply of oil is shrinking. That's why in the future cars may run on plain old vegetable oil. Here is a list of some oil alternatives that are being tested or are already being used to power car engines and other machines. Pass the deep fryer, please!

POWER	WHERE IT COMES FROM
Electricity	Batteries, solar and wind sources
Vegetable oil	Corn and other plant oils, used cooking oil
Hydrogen	Natural gas
Methanol	Alcohol
Ethanol	Distilled corn, barley, wheat
Bioethanol	Trees, grasses
Biodiesel	Blend of vegetable oil and diesel fuel
Propane	By-product of natural gas and oil refining

Hybrids to the Rescue!

If you're concerned about our overuse of oil and gas to power cars, consider a hybrid car. They combine an electric motor with a gas engine to greatly reduce gasoline use. Here's a list of hybrids sold in the United States:

Ford Escape Hybrid SUV • Honda Insight • Lexus GS450h • Toyota Camry Hybrid • Toyota Prius • Nissan Altima Hybrid • Mazda Tribute HEV

Deadliest Dinos

The movies have shown us some deadly dinosaurs, such as the *Tyrannosaurus rex* and *Velociraptor*, and how these meat-eating animals had to hunt, stalk, and chase their food. Their skeletons tell us that they were perfectly designed for these tasks. Sharp teeth and deadly claws made these dinosaurs among the deadliest (to other dinosaurs, anyway).

NAME	WHAT NAME MEANS	LENGTH (FT./M)
Allosaurus	Different reptile	40/12.2
Daspletosaurus	Frightful lizard	30/9.1
Deinonychus	Terrible claw	15/4.6
Dilophosaurus	Double-crested lizard	23/7
Eotyrannus	Dawn tyrant	16/4.9
Genusaurus	Knee lizard	13/4
Giganotosaurus	Giant southern lizard	42/12.5
Gorgosaurus	Fierce lizard	29.5/9
Megaraptor	Big plunderer	26/8
Neovenator	New hunter	25/7.6
Ornitholestes	Bird robber	7/2.1
Saurophaganax	Reptile-eating master	40/12.2
Tyrannosaurus	Tyrant reptile king	50/15.2
Utahraptor	Utah plunderer	19.5/5.9
Velociraptor	Swift robber	6.5/2

Mellowest Dinos

We assume these plant-eating dinosaurs spent long hours locating food and just grazing. Of course, no humans were around to check! Some of these plant-eaters were pretty fierce-looking, with horns and plates, but they just used them for defense. Here are some dinos that you could have kept as pets (if your backyard were as big as Wyoming).

NAME	WHAT IT MEANS	LENGTH (FT./M)
Antarctosaurus	Southern lizard	100/30.5
Apatosaurus	Deceptive reptile	90/27.4
Barosaurus	Heavy lizard	89/27.1
Brachiosaurus	Arm reptile	98/29.9
Diplodocus	Double beam	88/26.8
Hadrosaurus	Bulky lizard	25/7.6
Iguanodon	Iguana tooth	33/10.1
Lurdusaurus	Heavy lizard	29.5/9
Melanorosaurus	Black mountain lizard	40/12.2
Paralititan	Tidal giant	70/21.3
Sauroposeidon	Earthquake god lizard	98/29.9
Seismosaurus	Earthquake lizard	135/41.1
Supersaurus	Super lizard	110/33.5
Triceratops	Three-horned face	30/9
Vulcanodon	Vulcan's tooth	21/6.5

Rarest Plants
in the World

Many of these plants have become rare because their environments have changed or humans have destroyed them. It is estimated that one in eight species could become extinct. A few just don't reproduce fast enough to maintain great numbers, and some have just been discovered. Perhaps the rarest is *Encephalartos woodii*, also called wood cycad. It no longer exists in nature, and only the male species can be found in botanical gardens. A female species of this plant has never been found.

PLANT	LOCATION
Asian slipper orchid	Southwest Asia
Baker's larkspur	California
Daisy tree	Galapagos Islands
Desert yellowhead	Wyoming
Golden larch	Yangtze River Valley, China
Iris sofarana	Lebanon
Jellyfish tree	Seychelles
Lakeside daisy	Ohio
Metasequoia	China
Parachute penstemon	Colorado
Pink tickseed	Nova Scotia, Canada
Rosy periwinkle	Madagascar
Short's goldenrod	Indiana
Showy stickweed	Washington
Snowdonia hawkweed	Wales
Wollemi pines	Australia
Yukon-Whitlow grass	Yukon Territory, Canada

Stinky Plants

Most flowers smell pretty nice. In fact, people grow some of them, such as lilacs, just for their lovely scent. Then there are the plants listed here – the stinkiest, most awful-smelling plants in the world. The king of the stinky plants is the *Titan arum*, known as the corpse plant. Its odor is described as being like a rotting, dead human body, but when it blooms people rush to smell it – just to say they did! (We don't!) Enjoy these odors – if you dare!

Bear's foot hellebore

Corpse plant

Dragon lily

Durian fruit

Garlic

Ginkgo tree seeds

Hairy giant starfish flower

Onion

Ramps

Sauromatum

Skunk cabbage

Smelly socks grevillea

Smelly wallflower

Stinky rabbitbrush

Voodoo lily

Ditto!

Imagine coming face-to-face with your clone! Do you want someone to create another you, exactly like you? Sounds like science fiction, but for some animals it has become science fact. Scientists take DNA from one animal and "grow" an exact copy. Here are some of the animals that have been successfully cloned.

ANIMAL	NAME	LOCATION	YEAR
Sheep	Dolly	Scotland	1996
Mouse	Cumulina	USA	1997
Cow	2 unnamed calves	Japan	1998
Cow	George, Charlie	USA	1998
Rhesus monkey	Tetra	USA	1999
Wild sheep	Lamb	Italy	2000
Pig	Millie, Christa, Alexis, Carrel, Dotcom	USA	2000
Cat	Copycat	USA	2001
Pig	Noel, Angel, Star, Joy, Mary	Scotland	2001
Mule	Idaho Gem	USA	2003
Horse	Prometea	Italy	2003
Rat	Ralph	France	2003
Cat	Little Nicky	USA	2004
Horse	Pieraz Cryozootech Stallion	Italy	2005

A Really Tiny LIST

As tiny as the atom is, there are even smaller subatomic (smaller than an atom) particles. More than 300 subatomic particles have been identified. This list includes a few of those subatomic particles, from the biggest to the really, really, really, really, really, really smallest.

Atoms
> **Nucleus**
>> **Elementary Particles**
>>> **Quarks**
>>>> Up
>>>> Down
>>>> Strange
>>>> Charmed
>>>> Truth (top)
>>>> Beauty (bottom)
>>> **Leptons**
>>>> Electron
>>>> Electron Neutrino
>>>> Muon
>>>> Muon Neutrino
>>>> Tau
>>>> Tau Neutrino
>>> **Gauge Bosons**
>>>> Photon
>>>> Graviton
>>>> Gluon
>>>> Weakon
>> **Composite Particles (Hadrons)**
>>> **Mesons**
>>>> Pion
>>>> Kaon
>>>> Psi
>>>> Upsilon
>>> **Baryons**
>>>> Nucleon
>>>> Proton
>>>> Neutron
>>>> Hyperon
>>>> Lambda
>>>> Xi
>>>> Omega

Science
Game Page

Science is about connections, putting things together, and understanding how they interact and work together. In this game, you have to find connections between various things. Look at the three columns of words and create eight triple connections, using one term from each column. The words are all usually from related parts of one area of science. Plus, find the number in the fourth column that relates to the triple-connection you've made. The first one is done for you to show you how it works.

Andromeda	Math	Sheep	5
Ethanol	Tomography	Gas	115
Solar cells	Astronomy	Canine	10,000
Stratum corneum	Chemistry	Specimen	1985
Incisors	Botany	Power	0.3
Element	Electricity	Corn	GS450
Cloning	Power	Atlantis	1996
Eucalyptus	DNA	Doctor	32
Deca	Dermatology	Power	3-D
CAT	Dentistry	Dermis	435

CHAPTER FIVE

Words

In this chapter, read about a lot of good stuff, such as what to call *Bang!* and *Zip*, how to find the bathroom in China (and what to call it in ancient Israel), when you can write *Q* without a *U*, and how to Google. See? Good stuff.

THANKS TO THE
Greeks

The ancient Greeks gave our culture many things: democracy, drama, poetry, olive oil. They also left behind thousands of words that have been adopted into English. As you read this list, consider that you are actually reading Greek!

Alphabet*

Athlete

Cemetery

Diploma

Echo

Gymnasium

Hero

Mechanical

Museum

Mystery

Ocean

Olympics

Pylon

Rhythm

Stethoscope

Theater

Tragedy

*Alpha and beta are the first two Greek letters.

Here is what some planets would be named if Greek gods' names were used instead of Roman: Zeus (Jupiter), Cronos (Saturn), and Poseidon (Neptune). Remember the "old" planet Pluto? The Greek version would be Hades.

THANKS TO THE
Romans

Not long after the Greeks, the Romans came around and conquered much of the known world. They spread their language, Latin, throughout their empire. English takes many, many words and parts of words from Latin. The names of six planets — Mercury, Mars, Venus, Jupiter, Saturn, and Neptune — come from Roman gods. The signs of the zodiac are based on Latin terms. While many English words are based on Latin roots, some Latin words or terms remain unchanged in English. Here are a few well-known ones:

WORD/PHRASE	MEANING
Ad nauseum	Lasting way, way too long
Agenda	List of things to do, a schedule
Alumni	People who graduated from a particular school
Ante meridien (a.m.)	Before noon
Circa (c.)	About
Circus	Entertainment
i.e. (id est)	"That is"
Percent	Part of 100
Posse	Volunteer group that chases criminals
Post meridien (p.m.)	After noon
Postscript (P.S.)	A note after the main letter
Pro bono	For free
Subpoena	Legal term for a document calling a person to court
Versus (vs.)	Head-to-head, against
Vice versa	Back and forth, the same one way as another

Building the Alphabet

The present-day English alphabet has 26 letters, but where did they come from? Turns out that our English alphabet has many sources, but may have first originated from Semitic workers in Egypt, who created their own written shorthand. They passed it on to the Phoenicians, who in turn passed it on to the Greeks, who forwarded it to the Etruscans, who had it snatched away from them by the Romans. Whew! Most letters originally represented objects, but as different cultures adopted the symbols, the letters were turned, reversed, and changed. The Roman or Latin alphabet is closest to what we now use.

SOURCE/POSSIBLE ORIGINAL MEANING

A Greek, Roman/ox

B Greek, Roman/house

C Greek/camel

D Greek, Roman/door

E Greek, Roman/man

F Roman/hook

G Greek, Etruscan, Roman/camel

H Greek, Roman/fence

I   Greek, Roman/hand

J Roman/alternate form for I

K Greek, Roman/palm of the hand

L Greek, Roman/ox stick

M Greek, Roman/water

N Greek, Roman/snake

O Greek, Roman/eye

P Greek, Roman/mouth

Q Etruscan, Roman/monkey

R Roman/head

S Greek, Roman/tooth

T Greek, Roman/mark

U Roman/alternate form for V

V Etruscan/hook

W England/double u's

X Greek, Etruscan, Roman/fish

Y Greek/hook

Z Greek, Roman/weapon

SPEAKING "English"

The playwright George Bernard Shaw once said, "England and America are two countries divided by a common language." What he meant was that even though English is the language of both countries, the English of England is not like the English of America. The main difference these days is in slang. Here's a list of words that people in England use every day.

BRITISH ENGLISH	AMERICAN ENGLISH
Answerphone	Answering machine
Barrister	Lawyer
Bloke	Man
Bobby	Policeman
Brolly	Umbrella
Bum bag	Fanny pack
Chuffed	Proud or pleased
Crisps	Potato chips
Daft	Odd or kooky
Fairy cake	Cupcake
Fortnight	A period of two weeks
Gobsmacked	Amazed
Grotty	Gross
Knickers	Underwear
Knackered	Tired
Moggy	Alley cat
Oi!	Hey!
Petrol	Gasoline
Pushchair	Baby stroller
Queue	Line of waiting people
Sleeping policeman	Speed bump
Zed	The letter Z

Busiest Words

These English words occur most often in general use. The word *word* is the 45th most-used word (there, we just used it twice . . . wait, three times!). The word *list* is 310th on the, um, list.

the	it	are
of	you	with
to	that	as
and	he	I
a	was	his
in	for	they
is	on	

Top 10 Most-Used Verbs

is	be	were
was	have	use
are	had	said
	can	

Looking for the Loo

It's the bathroom. Or the washroom. Or the boys' room/girls' room. You and your family probably have your own names for it, too. You're not alone. Here is a list of other words used — yesterday or today — for this most useful of rooms.

Can
(American)

Head
(on board ships)

Jakes
(British)

John
(various)

Loo
(British)

House of Honor
(ancient Israel)

**House of
the Morning**
(ancient Egypt)

Necessarium
(ancient Rome)

Privy
(British)

Pot
(American)

Powder room
(American)

Restroom
(American)

Room 100
(popular in Europe)

Seat of ease
(medieval)

W.C.
(abbreviation for *water closet*)

ROOM 100

Really Gotta Go!

There's nothing worse than needing a bathroom — quick! — and not knowing how to ask. To help you avoid this potentially embarrassing problem, here's a list that tells you how to ask "Where is the bathroom?" in a variety of languages. Or you could just look for the signs.

LANGUAGE	"WHERE IS THE BATHROOM?"
Arabic	Ain Alhamaam?
Chinese	Cesuo zai nar?
Creole	Ki laplas twalét-la?
Dutch	Waar is het toilet?
French	Oú est les toilettes?
German	Wo ist die Toilette?
Hawaiian	Aia I hea ka lua?
Italian	Dov'é il bagno?
Japanese	Toire wa doko desu ka?
Latin	Ubi sunt loca secreta?
Polish	Gdzie jest toaleta?
Spanish	¿Donde está el baño?
Swahili	Choo kiko wapi?
Xhosa	Iphi indlu yangasese?
Yiddish	Vu iz de bodtsimer?

Mark It Up!

Do you ever get a paper back from your teacher and find that it's covered with the footprints of a wandering chicken? Well, we get our work back from our editor like that sometimes. Those scratches and marks and squiggles are really a secret code to improve your (and our) writing. On this list are some of the most common proofreaders' marks. The text on the bottom right shows how they all look on the page.

MARK   **MEANING**

ℰ Delete, which means remove

℮ Delete and close up (don't leave an empty space!)

Insert a space

∿ Switch places (the fancy word is *transpose*)

¶ Indent paragraph

ⓢⓟ Spell out this abbreviation

≡ Make a capital letter

/ Make a lower-case letter

Insert a hyphen

Insert a dash (longer than a hyphen)

Insert a comma

Insert an apostrophe

or Insert a period

Add quotation marks

Marks in Action!

The snarling beast must have weighed 900 lbs. and sported twenty-seven sharp teeth. I shivered in fear as it advanced toward me. "Hey, monster," i said. "How do you cut the ocean?" The riddle stopped it in its tracks. A confused look came over its face. The beasts teeth chattered — a frightening sound as it pondered answer. the "A sea saw!" I yelled. "Get it?" And then I sprinted for the mouth of the cave.

Old as the Hills

Have you ever heard of a simile [*SIM-ah-lee*]? It's a way of describing something by comparing it to something else, using the words *like* or *as*. That pizza was cold as ice. That elephant was as big as a house. Fred swam like a fish. Got it? Some of these comparisons are used way, way too often. When you see these, you know the writer got bored and couldn't think of a new way to say something. Try to avoid using these in your writing. If you do, you'll be as good as gold. (Oops, there's another one!)

Black as night
Busy as a bee
Cold as ice
Difficult as finding a needle in a haystack
Flies like a bird
Gentle as a lamb
Green as the grass
Hard as ice
Jumps like a kangaroo
Old as the hills
Neat as a pin
Nutty as a fruitcake

Pretty as a picture
Proud as a peacock
Quiet as a mouse
Runs like the wind
Shakes like a leaf
Sick as a dog
Sly as a fox
Smells like a skunk
Skinny as a rail
Slow as molasses
Spins like a top
Strong as an ox
Stubborn as a mule
Swims like a fish
Tall as a tree
Tough as nails
White as snow

Talking Sports

You might not know it, but you talk sports all the time. There are dozens a dozens of words, phrases, and expressions in English that come right fror the wide world of sports. See if you can think of others from each of thes sports. It's a whole new ball game, so we'll give you a sporting chance. If y can't think of any, though, well, that's just the way the ball bounces.

Baseball

Ballpark figure	Rough estimate
Bush league	Unprofessional or not very well done
Out of left field	From out of nowhere, unexpected
Right off the bat	Right away, immediately
Step up to the plate	Take your turn
Strike out	Fail
Throw a curve	Fool or surprise or bring up something unexpected

Basketball

The ball's in your court	It's your turn
Full court press	Give total effort, often from many people at once
Slam dunk	Easy to do

Boxing

Against the ropes   About to fail at something, running out of time

Throw in the towel   Give up or quit

Football

Huddle   Gather together

Make an end run   Avoid the regular way of doing things

Golf

You aced it!   You got it just right (from *ace*, a term for a hole in one)

Horse racing

Down to the wire   At the last minute, just in time

Kiss It Good-bye!

Baseball announcers often have their own special "home run call." Here's a short list of some famous ones:

"It might be, it could be . . . it is! A home run!" Harry Caray

"That ball is outta here!" John Sterling

"Open the window, Aunt Minnie! Here it comes!" Rosey Roswell

"Back, back, back, back . . . gone!" Chris Berman

"Going, going, gone! How about that?!" Mel Allen

Bang! Zip! Ding!

This was one of our favorite lists to write. You should have seen us tossing these words around the room: *Zing! Zap! Zoom!* What kind of words were we throwing? The term for words used to represent a sound is *onomatopoeia*. The idea of these words is to make you see in letters what you might hear with your ears. (By the way, comic books are a great place to see onomatopoeia in action.)

Bam!	Doink!	Tick-tock!
Bang!	Dong!	Splat!
Blam!	Fizz!	Wham!
Beep-beep!	Hiss!	Whap!
Boing!	Kaboom!	Whirr!
Clang!	Ka-ching!	Zip!
Clank!	Plop!	Zap!
Clunk!	Pop!	Zoom!
Ding!	Pow!	

Useful
Japanese Phrases

You might not know any Japanese — except maybe *sayonara* (good-bye) and Toyota, but here are some useful words and phrases to know if you ever find yourself in Tokyo. Of course, they are usually written in Japanese characters, so don't expect to see them written this way on a sushi menu in Japan.

ENGLISH	JAPANESE
Do you have this?	**Kore arimasu ka?** (pointing to the picture on the menu)
Excuse me.	**Sumimasen ga.**
Good morning.	**O-hayou gozai masu.**
Is there anyone there who can speak English?	**Sumimasen, eigo ga hanaseru kata irasshaimasu ka?**
My name is _____.	**Watashi no namae wa _____ desu.**
Please take me to a doctor.	**Oisha san ni tsurete itte kudasai.**
I'm sorry.	**Sumi masen.**
Thank you.	**Domo arigatou.**

We've used English letters here, but real Japanese uses characters. There are three sets: 46 *hiranga* that make up most of the basic "alphabet" of the language. There are thousands of *kanji* that represent sounds. Finally, *katakana* are used to write words from other languages in Japanese.

USEFUL
Chinese Phrases

Chinese is a language written with characters rather than an alphabet. That means each word is represented by one character. But there is an official way to spell out the sounds of the Chinese characters; it's called Pinyin. So here are some useful Chinese phrases, written in Pinyin. Because you never know — there might come a day when you need to introduce yourself in Chinese.

ENGLISH	CHINESE
Hello.	Ni hao.
My first name is ____, and my last name is ____.	Wo jiao ____ , xing ____.
I am a student.	Wo shi xuesheng.
I am an American.	Wo shi Meiguo ren.
Do you speak English?	Hui shuo Yingwen ma?
I like to eat Chinese food.	Wo xihuan chi Zong can.
How do you say ____ in Chinese?	____de Zhongwen zenme shuo?
Thank you.	Xie xie.
Good-bye.	Zai jian.

SECOND Languages

English is the dominant language spoken in the United States, but millions of people here speak more than one language. Some have learned that language in school, while others grew up in other countries and brought their native language to the United States with them. Here's a list of the languages with the greatest number of speakers in the United States.

LANGUAGE	APPROXIMATE NUMBER OF SPEAKERS
Spanish	28,100,000
Chinese	2,000,000
French	1,650,000
German	1,380,000
Tagalog	1,250,000
Vietnamese	1,000,000
Italian	1,000,000
Korean	895,000
Russian	710,000

¿Cómo Está Usted?

As you can see from the list on page 155, more Americans speak Spanish as a second language than any other. So these words and phrases might come in handy not only if you travel to a Spanish-speaking country, but if you visit many large cities in the United States. *¡Que bueno!*

ENGLISH	SPANISH
Do you speak English?	¿Habla inglés?
Good-bye.	Adios.
Hello.	Hola.
How are you?	¿Cómo está?
How old are you?	¿Cuantos años tiene?
How's it going?	¿Qué tal?
I am fine, thank you.	Estoy muy bien, gracias.
My name is _____.	Me llamo _____.
Thank you very much.	Muchas gracias.
What time is it?	¿Qué hora es?
Where is the _____?	¿Dónde está el/la_____?
You're welcome.	De nada.

Bonjour!

That's pronounced "bohn-ZHOOR!" and it's French for "Hello!" (It actually means "good day," but it's used like our "hello.") French is a very popular language around the world and many people know a few words of it. Here is a list of useful phrases for the next time you find yourself in Paris.

ENGLISH	FRENCH
Do you speak English?	Parlez-vous Anglais?
Hello.	Bonjour.
Good-bye.	Au revoir.
How are you?	Comment allez-vous?
I am fine, thank you.	Je suis bon, merci.
How old are you?	Quel âge avez-vous?
My name is ___.	Je m'appelle ___.
Thank you.	Merci.
What time is it?	Quelle heure est-íl?
Where is the ___?	Ou est le/la ___?
You're welcome.	De rien.

Just Added

Quiz time: Have all the English words we'll ever need been invented already? Nope. New words are being added to our language all the time (and no, they won't all be on your next vocabulary quiz . . . but you never know!). And older words get new meanings, too. The dictionary is the place where new words and definitions get the official stamp of approval. Here's a list of some of the phrases or words added to the *Merriam-Webster's Collegiate Dictionary* in 2005 and 2006.

Bludge   To avoid work or to sponge off someone else.

Brain freeze   A sudden shooting pain in the head caused by eating very cold food.

Cheesed off   Upset or angry (British)

Cybrarian   A person who deals with information on the Web, as opposed to in books.

Dead presidents   Slang term for money.

Def   Very cool.

Deke   Used in sports – to fake out or fool.

Frankenfood   Food that has been changed at the genetic level.

Goth   Rock music marked by dark lyrics; a fan of that music.

Hazmat   Short for *hazardous materials*.

Identity theft   The illegal use of someone else's name or personal information.

Manga   A popular Japanese form of animation.

Mosh pit   The area in front of a music stage where very rough dancing is done.

Mouse potato   A person who spends way, way, way too much time in front of their computer.

Ollie   A trick in skateboarding in which the rider pops the board off the ground.

Unibrow   When a person's eyebrows meet or nearly meet in the middle.

Words AT WORK

You might know some of these word-related terms, but then again, you might not! So here's a handy list of some useful types of words that will make your writing sing and your reading easier.

Antonyms Words that are opposite of one another. EXAMPLES: Big and small; rough and smooth

Homographs Words with the same spelling but different pronunciations and meanings. EXAMPLES: Bow (the front of a ship) and bow (as in bow and arrow)

Homophones Words with the same pronunciation but different meanings and spellings. EXAMPLES: To, too, two

Homonym Words spelled and pronounced the same, but with different meanings. EXAMPLES: quail (the bird) and quail (to cower in fear)

Synonym Words that are the same or nearly the same in meaning. EXAMPLES: Huge, enormous, gigantic

Oxymorons

No, these are not unintelligent folks breathing heavily. These are phrases whose words seem to contradict each other: jumbo shrimp, working vacation, small fortune. If it's a shrimp, for instance, how can it be jumbo (meaning huge)?

Looking It Up!

Have you ever asked your teacher or your parents what a word means? What do they usually say? That's right: "Look it up!" So when you go to the dictionary, what do you find? This list shows you the parts of a dictionary definition, based on the example of a word that you'll be familiar with: *goofy*.

goofy\gü-fē*adj* **goof·i·er**; **-est** (1921): being crazy, ridiculous, or mildly ludicrous: silly— **goof·i·ly**\-fə-lē\ *adv* — **goof·i·ness**\-fē-nəs*n*

A The word itself, often in boldface.

B How to pronounce the word; there are lots of funny ways that letters are written in these pronunciations – ask for help!

C The part of speech.

D The word with its suffixes, in this case to make *goofiest*.

E The year the word was first used in this way in English.

F The definition.

G Other forms of the word that are different parts of speech, along with their own pronunciations and parts of speech.

Getting It Started

Who wrote the first dictionary of English? No one's exactly sure, but one candidate is a gent named Robert Cawdrey, who put together a long list of words in 1604. English writer Samuel Johnson's 1755 dictionary is without a doubt the best to that point. Noah Webster (yup, he was a real guy) published the first American dictionary in 1806.

Sneaky Smack

Here are some fun ideas for sneaky ways to "give someone the business." Always nice to add a vocabulary lesson to your activities on the playground, right? (Note: Say all of these with a smile on your face!)

"Wow, Joan, that perfume you're wearing is perfectly odiferous!"
(*Odiferous* means it smells bad.)

"Nice going, Bob. Your halitosis is really working well today."
(*Halitosis* is a word that means bad breath.)

"Gee, Dan, I wish I could be a great ruminant like you."
(Use this on someone chewing gum; a *ruminant* is an animal, such as a cow, that chews its cud.)

"Ha-ha, that's a good one. Your jokes always make me somnambulate."
(*Somnambulate* means to sleepwalk.)

"That dress you're wearing has a real consanguinity with one my grandma wore."
(*Consanguinity* means having a close relation or connection to.)

Q's Without U's

One of the most famous spelling rules is that the letter Q is always followed by the letter U. Well, we're here to tell you that rule was made to be broken! As any good Scrabble® player knows, there are dozens of words that have a Q in them that is *not* followed by a U. Most come from other languages, such as Arabic or Chinese, but have been accepted into some English or Scrabble® dictionaries. Here's a short list of rule-breaking words.

Burqa
A garment worn by some Muslim women that covers the face and body

Qadi
A Muslim judge

Qaid
A type of government official in Muslim countries

Qat
A type of shrub found in the Middle East

Qintar
The name of the money used in Albania

Qiviut
The wool on the underside of a musk ox

Qoph
The 19th letter of the Hebrew alphabet

Qwerty
The layout of standard computer keyboards and typewriters

Tranqs
Short for tranquilizers, special drugs that help patients sleep

Umiaq
A word from the Inuit that means "kayak"

How 2 Txt Msg

IMHO, text messaging has become an enormous worldwide communications phenomenon. Billions of text messages are sent around the world — and across the classroom. Most are sent by cell phones, but people can also use other small handheld devices. With a tiny screen and even tinier keys, cell phones are not cut out for writing really long letters. A system of abbreviations has been developed to make texting easier and faster. These are different from the "emoticons," or little faces that people make out of various punctuation marks. Here are some of the most well-known text-only abbreviations.

AFAIK	As far as I know
B4	Before
BCNU	Be seein' you
BRB	Be right back
CM	Call me
F2F	Face to face
IMHO	In my humble opinion
JK	Just kidding
L8R	Later
LOL	Laughing out loud
OBTW	Oh, by the way
ROTFL	Rolling on the floor laughing
T+	Think positive
TTFN	Ta-ta for now
TX	Thanks
WTG	Way to go!

Aloha, Hawaii!

Hawaii is one of the 50 states, of course, but it used to be an independent kingdom. Many words from that language are still used regularly on the islands, by tourists and locals alike. In recent years, many people have worked hard to learn the native Hawaiian language. A fun bit of language trivia is that there are only 12 letters in the Hawaiian alphabet: *A, E, H, I, K, L, M, N, O, P, U, W*. Here's a list of some familiar — and not-so-familiar — Hawaiian words.

HAWAIIAN	ENGLISH
Ae	Yes
Aloha	Hello or good-bye
Hula	Dance
Kai	Ocean
Kahakai	Beach
Kane	Man
Keiki	Child or baby
Lei	Flower garland
Luau	Feast
Mahalo	Thank you
Moku	Island
Nani	Beautiful
Pipi	Cow
Ukelele	Small guitar
Wahine	Woman
Wiwi	Skinny

Super
Search Tricks

Using a search engine on the Internet is a great way to find information you need (or to find that video of the kid with a pie on his head or something). But there's more to using a search engine than just typing in a word or two. Here are some tips that work on most search engines and can help you find what you need more quickly and more accurately. Make sure it's okay with your folks before you start working on the Internet.

Books

The Google® site has millions of books in its servers. Type in *book* followed by your search term.

Calculator

Either from the search engine's main page or as the top answer to searching this word, you should get to a site that works like a regular desktop calculator. You can also, on some engines, type in a calculation and it will figure it for you.

Conversion

While we hope you use the chart on page 116, you can use search engines to convert English to metric measurements (and vice versa) or convert currencies. Type in something like "47 in. in cm" and you'll get 47 in. = 119.38 cm.

Hyphen

Want to eliminate some search results? Use the "-" symbol. For example, if you wanted to look for sites relating to Turkey the nation and not turkey the oh-so-tasty bird, you could type in "turkey-Thanksgiving" or "turkey-bird."

Intitle

Put the word *intitle* before your search term, and what you'll get are only Web sites with that term as part of the title. Using *intext* instead searches for the term in the page, not in the Web site title.

Phone listings

Need to find a friend's phone number? Try typing their name (or family name) and address into the search box; if they have a listed number, it should come up. On some engines, you need to type *phonebook:* before the name.

Q&A

Find quick answers to basic questions by just asking the question. The answer will come first and include the place where they got it. Type in "population of Greenland," and you'll get "56,375" and perhaps a link to the CIA World Fact Book to check it.

Spelling/Definition

Type the word as best you can (*busines*, for example) and hit search. In most engines, the proper spelling will come up with something like "Did you mean 'business'?" Or type in *define* followed by the word and a definition will come up.

Weather

Type *weather* before a city or location and you'll get a forecast for that area.

Words
Game Page

We'll go with a classic here — a crossword puzzle. You know the drill; read the clues and fill in the blanks. You can find answers to most of the clues within the chapter if you get stuck.

Across

1. Football term for going around something

5. Shortest most popular verb

7. What a word means

10. New dictionary word for something "new" to eat

11. Greek word for a place to sweat

Down

2. Where the words live

3. Good _____

4. Slang term for bathroom

6. Slang term for bathroom, or "kick the _____"

8. Really short popular word

9. A "loo" is a bath_____.

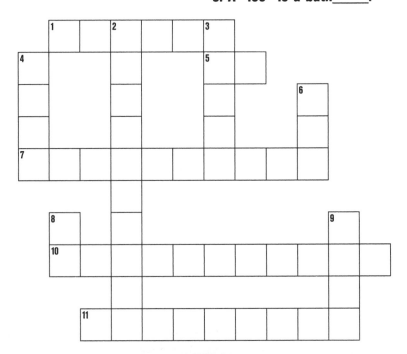

CHAPTER SIX

Pop Culture

What is pop culture? Pretty much everything except homework. If you can watch it, read it, listen to it, dance to it, download it, or just stare at it, you might find it in here.

BEFORE
You Heard of Them

Many entertainers got their first big break in show business in typical ways. For instance, Jennifer Lopez got her start as a dancer on the TV show *In Living Color*. Britney Spears, Justin Timberlake, and Christina Aguilera all wore Mouseketeer ears on *The Mickey Mouse Club* before they became world-famous. But for lots of stars, their first jobs had nothing to do with "showbiz." Look at this list of first jobs of the rich and famous.

CELEB	FIRST JOB
Jennifer Aniston	Waitress
Garth Brooks	Boot salesman
Mariah Carey	Hat checker
Jim Carrey	Factory worker
Coolio	Firefighter
Danny DeVito	Hairdresser
Harrison Ford	Carpenter
Faith Hill	Secretary
Madonna	Dunkin' Donuts counter girl
Demi Moore	Debt collector
Jack Nicholson	Mail sorter
Brad Pitt	Refrigerator mover
Jerry Seinfeld	Lightbulb salesman
Robin Williams	Street mime

Great Song, Curtis!

Curtis James Jackson III is one of the world's most popular hip-hop stars. Christopher Bridges sells tons of CDs and makes fans go crazy. Dana Owens is a musical and movie star. What do you *mean* you've never heard of any of these folks? Well, you have, just not by those names. Most rap and hip-hop stars go by childhood nicknames earned before they were famous. Why use the nicknames? Because Earl and Martin and Howard and Kimberly just don't sound phat.

RAP NAME	REAL NAME
Busta Rhymes	Trevor Tahiem Smith
Cassie	Casandra Ventura
Coolio	Artis Ivey, Jr.
Dr. Dre	Andre Romel Young
Eminem	Marshall Bruce Mathers
Fifty Cent	Curtis James Jackson III
Funkmaster Flex	Aston George Taylor, Jr.
Ice Cube	Oshea Jackson
Jam Master Jay	Jason William Mizell
Jay-Z	Shawn Corey Carter
Lil' Kim	Kimberly Denise Jones
Ludacris	Christopher Bridges
Nelly	Cornell Hayes, Jr.
Pimp C	Chad Butler
Puff Daddy (a.k.a. Diddy)	Sean John Combs
Queen Latifah	Dana Owens
Shawnna	Rashawnna Guy
Snoop Dogg	Cordazer Calvin Broadus
T.I.	Clifford Harris, Jr.

Top Country
GROUPS

Country music is the top-selling type of popular music in the United States. And some country singers like to make beautiful music together. These groups are the tops in country music right now, according to the BMG Country Music Club.

Alabama
Blackhawk
Brooks & Dunn
Diamond Rio
Dixie Chicks
Lonestar
The Mavericks
Montgomery Gentry
Rascal Flatts

Great Group Efforts

The bestselling album of all time by a country group is *Wide Open Spaces* by the Dixie Chicks. It was released in 1998 and sold 8 million copies by December 1999. Within a year of release, the record went quadruple platinum and earned a Grammy for Best Country Album.

Top Country
SOLO ACTS

Whether it's in the shower or on the stage, some people just like to sing alone. These solo singers are the tops in country music right now, according to the BMG Country Music Club. Of course, they still have bands behind them. It's just that these folks get all the credit.

Trace Adkins

Clint Black

Kenny Chesney

Martina McBride

Reba McIntre

Willie Nelson

Brad Paisley

Leann Rimes

Josh Turner

Carrie Underwood

Keith Urban

Hank Williams, Jr.

Hottest Album

The bestselling country album of all time is Shania Twain's *Come On Over*. It was released in 1997 and has since sold a record 39 million copies worldwide as of January 2006. The record remains a big seller.

No. 1 in No. 1s

It's a big deal to get to the No. 1 spot on *Billboard Magazine*'s Hot 100 chart, and very few artists have done it more than once. Even fewer have done it more than 10 times. And once you're up there, it's hard to stay. Here are some singers who have done it. This list covers songs released from January 1, 1955, to the present.

Artists with the Most No. 1 Hits

The Beatles	20
Elvis Presley	17
Mariah Carey	17
Michael Jackson	13
The Supremes	12
Madonna	12
Whitney Houston	11

Artists with the Most Weeks at No. 1

Elvis Presley	80 weeks
Mariah Carey	77 weeks
The Beatles	59 weeks
Boyz II Men	50 weeks
Usher	40 weeks
Michael Jackson	37 weeks

How CDs Are Made

What's as thin as a stick of gum but holds more than an hour of music? A CD, of course. That little plastic disc is just 4/100ths of an inch (1.2 mm) thick. How do they get all that stuff onto something so thin? The answer is that every CD has five layers. Here's what they are and what they do.

1 An injection-molded clear polycarbonate plastic layer accounts for the majority of the CD's thickness and weight. It protects the data layer from damage on the play side, and also acts as a lens to focus the CD player's laser onto the data layer.

2 The clear plastic layer is molded or pressed with microscopic bumps arranged as a single, continuous, extremely long spiral track. This is the data layer, where the music and any other information is stored. It's the layer that the CD player reads.

3 A thin, reflective aluminum layer lies on top of the data layer. It acts like a mirror. The CD player shines a laser onto the data bumps; the light is reflected back to the detector in the CD player by this shiny layer.

4 An ultra-thin plastic coating is added to protect the reflective and data layers. It also forms a surface for the label layer.

5 The label layer is printed on top of the protective layer. This is the part that tells you what's on the CD.

How Big Is a Bump?

The spiral track on the data layer circles from the inside of the disc to the outside. The elongated bumps that make up the track are each about 0.5 microns wide (a micron is a millionth of a meter) and 125 nanometers high (a nanometer is a billionth of a meter). That's incredibly tiny, but the track itself is very long. If you could lift the data track off a CD and stretch it out, it would be almost 3.5 miles (5 km) long!

With the Band

When large rock, hip-hop, or country bands go out on tour, they take along a bunch of helpers called "roadies" (short for road crew). Roadies travel with the musicians and handle every part of the tour and the show except for actually playing the music. They often do a lot of different things, but some roadies have very specific jobs. Here are a few of them.

FOH engineer FOH stands for "front of house." This is the sound technician who sits out in the audience, often behind a big electronics board, adjusting all the speakers, amps, and microphones so they sound just right.

Guitar tech This is the only person who is allowed to handle a musician's guitars. He orders supplies such as picks and strings; maintains and repairs guitars, amplifiers, and cables; restrings, cleans, and tunes the guitars; sets up all the guitars and their equipment on the stage; and retunes or restrings a guitar during a performance, if necessary.

Instrument techs Bass players, drummers, and keyboard players may also have technicians whose only job is to keep the instruments working properly and make sure they are set up onstage. This can include details like making sure a special lucky stuffed animal is sitting in a certain place on a certain keyboard.

Lighting techs Lighting technicians are involved with setting up and controlling lighting equipment for the club or arena where the band plays.

Pyrotechnics/SFX Explosions, flashes, smoke, or flames on stage are called pyrotechnics, and these guys set them all up. SFX stands for "special effects," and the SFX guys may also coordinate with the lighting techs and the stage manager for other kinds of special effects.

Security Keeping the musicians safe and making sure nobody barges in on them is the main job of these guys. They also make sure no one gets up on the stage during a concert.

Sound techs These guys set up, test, and operate the sound equipment, and select, place, and adjust microphones. They may also operate controls to maintain correct sound levels and introduce prerecorded special effects during the show.

Stage manager The stage manager organizes the concert, making sure all the other roadies and technicians know what their jobs are.

Steel dogs This is the crew who builds those tall steel towers for shows at stadiums.

Tour manager This person organizes the schedule the group will follow, including what venues they will play at, who will go along with the band, what hotels they'll stay at, and how they will get from place to place.

Truss spotlight operators These are the guys who sit in the lighting truss (a set of pipes and brackets that hold up the many lights) above the stage with a safety belt holding them in their chairs. They hit the performers with a spotlight from above and behind.

Get a Grip!

In a movie, the producer, the director, the actors — and sometimes the costume designers — get all the attention and win all the Oscars. But there are a lot of other cool movie jobs that won't make you famous. Here are some of them.

Best boy The second person in charge of any group, most commonly the chief assistant to the gaffer (see below); women can be best boys.

Body double Takes the place of the actor for a specific scene, usually because their body has a characteristic that the actor lacks, such as big muscles or pretty feet.

Boom operator Holds the boom microphone (a microphone attached to the end of a long pole) out over the actors.

Camera loader Operates the clapboard, signaling the beginning of a shot, and also loads the film into the film magazines.

Continuity coordinator Takes photographs of every scene to make sure the actors always are wearing the right clothing or have the right props the next time a similar scene is shot.

Dialogue coach Helps an actor's speech fit their character, usually by assisting with pronunciation and accents.

Foley artist Creates incidental sound effects, such as footsteps and other noises, in a film.

Gaffer In charge of the electrical department.

Grip Maintains and positions equipment on a set; the dolly grip positions the small truck that rolls along tracks and carries the camera, cameraperson, and occasionally the director; the key grip is in charge of a group of grips.

Wrangler Responsible for the care and control of all animals on the set; there are also "baby wranglers," who help keep track of child or infant actors.

Dig These DVDs

Don't you just love to see a great movie over and over? The fact that you know what happens next and what everyone is going to say is part of the fun. These are the top 10 bestselling DVDs on Amazon.com over the past 10 years.

1 *The Lord of the Rings: The Fellowship of the Ring*

2 *The Lord of the Rings: The Two Towers*

3 *The Lord of the Rings: The Return of the King*

4 *Star Wars**

5 *The Matrix*

6 *Finding Nemo*

7 *Harry Potter and the Sorcerer's Stone*

8 *Pirates of the Caribbean: The Curse of the Black Pearl*

9 *Gladiator*

10 *Shrek*

*Boxed set of Episodes 4 – 6

Spy Guys & Gals

Some of the most popular — and coolest! — characters in movies and on TV are spies! Their exploits amaze and entertain us — and sometimes make us laugh. They have the best "toys," they drive the coolest cars, and they sneak into the most sneakproof places. Through it all, they remain smooth and easygoing. We asked an expert on movie and TV spies to give us a list of 10 of the most popular, coolest, most fun movie and TV spies of all time.

1. James Bond
Getting his gadgets from Q and his assignments from M, British Agent 007 — cinema's most famous spy — has saved the world from criminal masterminds in 21 movies since 1962. Six actors have played Bond on the big screen.

2. Austin Powers
A satire of James Bond, Mike Myers's comic spy Austin Powers was frozen in the 1960s so he could be defrosted in the 1990s to defeat the criminal plans of Dr. Evil. Myers played both characters in three Austin Powers movies (1997–2002).

3. The Spy Kids
Carmen and Juni Cortez are young spies who helped their secret-agent parents battle evildoers in three *Spy Kids* adventure films (2001–03).

4. The Impossible Missions Force
Jim Phelps is the master spy who, with his team of specialists, carried out "impossible missions" for the U.S. government in the CBS-TV series *Mission: Impossible* (1966–73). Decades later, Tom Cruise produced and starred in three feature films loosely based on this hit spy show.

5. Napoleon Solo & Illya Kuryakin
These cool spies were once as popular as The Beatles. Solo and Illya were agents for the top secret U.N.C.L.E. organization, which, from 1964 to 1968 on NBC, battled Thrush, a worldwide conspiracy intent on taking over the world.

7. Cody Banks
In the *Agent Cody Banks* movies (2003–04), Frankie Muniz played a teenage kid who is

recruited by the CIA to use his skateboarding and snowboarding skills – along with some cool gadgets – to carry out secret missions.

8. Maxwell Smart & Agent 99

In the classic TV comedy *Get Smart* (1965–70), Max was the bumbling Agent 86 who, with the beautiful Agent 99, carried out assignments for the Chief of Control to stop the mean and rotten spies of Kaos. Every time Max messed up, you could be sure he'd say, "Sorry about that, Chief!" – a phrase that became popular all over the United States.

9. James West & Artemus Gordon

On the clever CBS-TV series *The Wild Wild West* (1965–69), U.S. Secret Service agents West and Gordon used gadgets, disguises, and their private train to battle villains in the days of the American West.
The show was remade into a movie starring Will Smith in 1999.

10. Kelly Robinson & Alexander Scott

In the groundbreaking NBC-TV show *I Spy* (1965–68), Kelly and Scott were U.S. agents who carried out their undercover missions by traveling the world as a tennis player and his trainer. The first American TV series to co-star an African-American (Bill Cosby), *I Spy* was remade in 2002 into a comedy film starring Eddie Murphy and Owen Wilson.

CELEBRITY
Kids' Book Authors

Madonna has done it five times and Jamie Lee Curtis has done it seven. NFL stars have done it along with country music singers. What are they all doing? Writing children's books. It's become a hot thing among celebrities to write kids' books. Here are some celebrities who have published books for little kids.

Jason Alexander — *Dad, Are You the Tooth Fairy?*

Tiki Barber and Ronde Barber — *By My Brother's Side*

Katie Couric — *The Blue Ribbon Day, The Brand New Kid*

Billy Crystal — *I Already Know I Love You*

Jamie Lee Curtis — *Today I Feel Silly, Is There Really a Human Race?, I'm Gonna Like Me, Where Do Balloons Go?, It's Hard to be Five, When I Was Little, Tell Me Again About the Night I Was Born*

Whoopi Goldberg — *Alice*

Mia Hamm — *Winners Never Quit!*

Jay Leno — *If Roast Beef Could Fly*

John Lithgow — *I'm a Manatee, The Remarkable Farkle McBride, Marsupial Sue, Carnival of the Animals*

Madonna — *The English Roses, Lotsa de Cashsa, The Adventures of Abdi, Mr. Peabody's Apples, Yakov and the Seven Thieves*

Dolly Parton — *Coat of Many Colors*

Jerry Seinfeld — *Halloween*

John Travolta — *Propeller One-Way Night Coach*

Kid Authors

The classic story *Frankenstein* was written in 1818 by Mary Shelley when she was just 19 years old. But she was certainly not the youngest person to write a book. If you like to write, think about these kids who wrote books when they were even younger than Shelley. We'd love to have you on this list next time we get around to updating this book!

Gil C. Alicea/16
The Air Down Here: True Tales From a South Bronx Boyhood

Amelia Atwater-Rhodes/13
In the Forests of the Night

Charlotte Brontë/13
The Search After Happiness

Zlata Filipovic/13
Zlata's Diary: A Child's Life in Wartime Sarajevo

Anne Frank/14
Diary of a Young Girl

Miles Franklin/16
My Brilliant Career

Latoya Hunter/12
Diary of Latoya Hunter: My First Year in Junior High

S.E. Hinton/16
The Outsiders

Gordon Korman/12
This Can't Be Happening at McDonald Hall

Megan McNeil Libby/16
Postcards From France

Dave Lindsay/14
Dave's Quick and Easy Web Pages

Christopher Paolini/15
Eragon

Who's Who in

If you read *Harry Potter and the Sorcerer's Stone, The Chamber of Secrets, The Prisoner of Azkaban, The Goblet of Fire, The Order of the Phoenix, The Half-Blood Prince*, and *The Deathly Hallows*, you know the wizarding universe has grown pretty large. Here's a handy guide to the major characters.

The Potters

Harry Potter
James and Lily Potter, Harry's parents
Vernon and Petunia Dursley, Harry's muggle uncle and aunt
Dudley Dursley, Harry's muggle cousin

Harry's School Friends

Ron Weasley
Hermione Granger
Neville Longbottom
Parvati Patil
Padma Patil

Luna Lovegood
Fred Weasley
George Weasley
Ginny Weasley

Harry's School Enemies

Draco Malfoy   **Vincent Crabbe**   **Gregory Goyle**

Hogwarts Teachers

Albus Dumbledore, headmaster
Filius Flitwick, charms
Minerva McGonagall, transfiguration
Horace Slughorn, potions
Severus Snape, potions, defense against the dark arts
Pomona Sprout, herbology
Gilderoy Lockhart, defense against the dark arts

Harry Potter

Argus Filch, caretaker
Rubeus Hagrid, care of mystical creatures
Madam Hooch, flying
Aurora Sinistra, astronomy
Sybill Patricia Trelawney, divination
Wilhelmina Grubbly-Plank, care of magical creatures

Other Wizards

Sirius Black, Order of the Phoenix
Remus Lupin, Order of the Phoenix
Alastor Moody, Order of the Phoenix
Lord Voldemort (real name Tom Marvolo Riddle)
Bellatrix Lestrange, follower of Voldemort
Lucius Malfoy, follower of Voldemort
Peter Pettigrew, follower of Voldemort
Dolores Umbridge, follower of Voldemort
Quirinus Quirrell, follower of Voldemort
Cornelius Fudge, Minister of Magic
Rufus Scrimgeour, Minister of Magic
Arthur and Molly Weasley, Ron's parents
Charlie, Bill, and Percy Weasley, Ron's grown brothers

Other Creatures

Dobby, house-elf at Hogwarts
Kreacher, house-elf at Hogwarts
Hedwig, Harry's owl
Pigwidgeon, Ron's owl

Crookshanks, Hermione's cat
Mrs. Norris, Argus Filch's cat
Scabbers, Ron's rat

What's That Cell?

There are about 203 million cell phone users in the United States, and about 2 billion worldwide. Seven out of 10 kids age 16 or 17 own cell phones, compared to half of kids ages 14 and 15 and one-fourth of all 13-year-olds. Eighty-three percent of teens with cells use them every day, and what they do with them is very different from what adults do. Here are some of the results of a Pew Research Center survey showing what teens and young adults are more likely than older adults to do with their cell phones.

* Personalize their cell phone by changing wallpaper or adding ring tones.
* Make cell phone calls to fill up their free time or while waiting for someone.
* Not be truthful about where they are when talking on their cell phone.
* Use their cell phone for text messaging.
* Use their cell phone to take pictures.
* Use their cell phone to play games.
* Use their cell phone to access the Internet.

The most popular non-voice feature is text messaging; more than 2.5 billion text messages are sent each month, mostly by teens and young adults. Almost two of every three people have also used their cell phone backlight to look for something in the dark.

Star Barkers

Snoop Dogg keeps Siamese cats. Other celebrity cat lovers include Regis Philbin, Martha Stewart, Kirsten Dunst, Jay Leno, Christina Ricci, Leeza Gibbons, Billy Crystal, and Lisa Loeb. Matt LeBlanc has a pet lizard, and Jacob Underwood from O-Town has a monkey named Abbey. But by far the most visible and most popular celebrity pets are dogs. And when it comes to dogs, those tiny Chihuahuas are really big. Here are some canines of the rich and famous.

CELEBRITY	DOG
Jessica Alba	2 Pugs
Jessica Biel	Bulldog
Jim Carrey	Great Dane
Hilary Duff	Chihuahua
David Duchovny	Collie-Terrier mix
Brett Favre	Yorkshire Terrier
Wayne Gretzky	Dachshund
Janet Jackson	Chow Chow, Mixed breed
Ashley Judd	Cockapoo
Stephen King	Pembroke Welsh Corgi
Jude Law	Mixed breed
Madonna	Chihuahua
Kelly Osborne	Puggle
Pink	Mixed breed
Adam Sandler	Bulldog
Jessica Simpson	Maltipoo
Will Smith	2 Rottweilers
Britney Spears	Chihuahua
Oprah Winfrey	2 Amer. Cocker Spaniels
Kristi Yamaguchi	Toy Rat Terrier

Kids' Choice Champs

People don't ask kids what they think about stuff nearly enough. One exception is Nickelodeon; every year, the cable TV network asks kids to vote for their favorite movies, TV shows, music, and famous people. In April 2006, they had their 19th Kids' Choice Awards. The show always features lots of celebrity guests, musical acts (New Kids on the Block — trust us, they were famous at the time — provided the first musical performance for a Kids' Choice Awards show), and plenty of slime.

	2006	2005
TV Show	*Drake & Josh*	*American Idol*
TV Actress	Jamie Lynn Spears	Raven Symone
TV Actor	Drake Bell	Romeo
Movie	*Harry Potter and the Goblet of Fire*	*The Incredibles*
Movie Actor	Will Smith	Adam Sandler
Movie Actress	Lindsay Lohan	Hilary Duff
Animated Movie	*Madagascar*	*The Incredibles*
Voice from an Animated Movie	Chris Rock (*Madagascar*)	Will Smith (*Shark Tale*)
Cartoon	*SpongeBob SquarePants*	*SpongeBob SquarePants*

	2006	2005
Athlete	**Lance Armstrong**	**Tony Hawk**
Female Singer	**Kelly Clarkson**	**Avril Lavigne**
Male Singer	**Jesse McCartney**	**Usher**
Music Group	**Green Day**	**Green Day**
Song	**"Wake Me Up When September Ends" (Green Day)**	**"Burn" (Usher)**
Book Series	***Harry Potter***	***A Series of Unfortunate Events***
Video Game	**Madagascar: Operation Penguin**	**Shrek 2**

The Wannabe Award

The Wannabe Award is given every year to the celebrity kids most want to be like. Here are some recent winners:

1997	Will Smith	2002	Janet Jackson
1998	Tia and Tamera Mowry	2003	Will Smith
1999	Jonathan Taylor Thomas	2004	Adam Sandler
2000	Rosie O'Donnell	2005	Queen Latifah
2001	Tom Cruise	2006	Chris Rock

POP CULTURE

Your TV Faves!

Like watching TV? These are the most popular kids' shows that are still on today, according to TV.com. How many of them have you seen?

SHOW NAME	FIRST YEAR ON THE AIR
1. *Power Rangers*	1993
2. *American Dragon: Jake Long*	2005
3. *LazyTown*	2004
4. *Thomas the Tank Engine & Friends*	1984
5. *Sesame Street*	1969
6. *15/Love*	2004
7. *Mike's Super-Short Show*	2003
8. *Blue's Clues*	1996
9. *Flight 29 Down*	2005
10. *Mew Mew Power*	2005

? Quick: Without looking at the next sentence, what are the colors used by the main Power Rangers? Tick, tick, tick . . . time's up! Yellow, blue, red, pink, green, black, and white. The hit show began life as an all-Japanese production. In 1993, Saban Entertainment combined new English-language sections with the the original Japanese martial arts parts to create a new show.

Cool Cartoons

What goes better with Saturday morning than cartoons? Of course, cartoons go pretty well with just about any morning . . . or afternoon . . . or evening. These are the most popular animated shows in the 21st century, according to TV.com.

	SHOW NAME	YEARS ON THE AIR
1.	*SpongeBob SquarePants*	1999–
2.	*Justice League Unlimited*	2001–
3.	*Teen Titans*	2003–
4.	*Futurama*	1999–2003
5.	*FullMetal Alchemist*	2004–
6.	*Yu-Gi-Oh!*	2001–
7.	*Dragonball Z*	1996–2003
8.	*The Fairly OddParents*	2001–
9.	*Invader ZIM*	2001–2002
10.	*The Adventures of Jimmy Neutron*	2002–

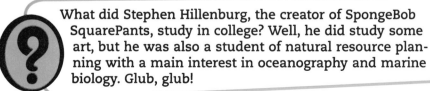

? What did Stephen Hillenburg, the creator of SpongeBob SquarePants, study in college? Well, he did study some art, but he was also a student of natural resource planning with a main interest in oceanography and marine biology. Glub, glub!

Who's Who in
The Simpsons

The Simpsons began life in 1987 as one-minute cartoons on *The Tracey Ullman Show*. They were created by cartoonist Matt Groening, and became a weekly series in 1989. Now, *The Simpsons* is the longest-running animated series in the history of television. A lot of characters have come and gone in all those years. Here are some of them.

The Simpson Family

Homer Simpson, father

Marge Simpson, mother

Bart Simpson, son

Lisa Simpson, daughter

Maggie Simpson, baby daughter

Abe and Mona Simpson, Homer's parents

Jacqueline and Clancy Bouvier, Marge's parents

Selma and Patty Bouvier, Marge's twin sisters

Springfield Residents

Comic Book Guy, owner, Android's Dungeon

Charles Montgomery "Monty" Burns, owner of Springfield Nuclear Power Plant

Carl Carlson, Homer's coworker

Ned Flanders, Simpsons' next-door neighbor

Rod and Todd, Ned's sons

Groundskeeper Willie, school groundskeeper

Barney Gumble, regular at Moe's Tavern

Dr. Julius Hibbert, physician

Edna Krabappel, fourth-grade teacher

Krusty the Klown, TV celebrity

Lenny Leonard, Homer's coworker

Timothy Lovejoy, reverend of First Church of Springfield

Nelson Muntz, school bully

Apu Nahasapeemapetilon, owns the Kwik-E-Mart

Manjula Nahasapeemapetilon, Apu's wife

Poonam, Sashi, Pria, Uma, Anoop, Sandeep, Nabendu, Gheet, the Nahasapeemapetilon children

Sherri and Terri, purple-haired twins

Seymour Skinner, Spingfield Elementary School principal

Agnes Skinner, Seymour's mother

Waylon Smithers, Jr., Mr. Burns's assistant

Cletus and Brandine Delroy, country folks

Mo Szyslak, owner of Moe's Tavern

Milhouse Van Houten, Bart's best friend

Clancy Wiggum, chief of police

Ralph Wiggum, school idiot

Matt Groening's real father is named Homer and his mother is named Margaret. He also has two sisters, Lisa and Maggie. He says he named the main character Bart because it is an anagram of *brat.* What's an anagram? It's a new word made by mixing up the letters of another word.

TV Firsts

We know, we know . . . you don't watch a lot of TV. You're a reader, an athlete, an artist . . . you don't need the boob tube. Yeah . . . right. C'mon, admit it; you love TV. We do! (Though we shouldn't overdo it.) We could probably do a whole book on lists of TV things like shows, actors, awards, etc. But here we'll flick the switch on TV history and give you this list of cool TV firsts, without which you'd just be staring at an empty box instead of a TV (and with some of the stuff on TV these days, an empty box might be better!).

First TV broadcast
J. L. Baird and Charles Jenkins combined their own work with that of earlier inventors (such as Karl Braun and Paul Nipkow) to transmit the first (fuzzy!) pictures in 1926.

First workable TV transmission device
Philo T. Farnsworth built on the work of other scientists and added his own twists to land a spot as the "inventor" of television, with the creation of his machine in 1930.

First TV program
This unnamed show of music, speeches, and comics was aired on July 21, 1931. Since only a few people had TVs, it didn't get great ratings!

First animated TV show
Crusader Rabbit debuted in 1949.

First successful color TV
This was invented in 1941 by scientists at Bell Labs. *Walt Disney's World of Color* was the first color TV show, in 1961.

First TV dinner
Dig in and watch! The Swanson Company first sold these in 1953.

First remote control
Thank goodness! Couch potatoes everywhere rejoiced when Robert Adler invented this in 1956.

First satellite dish
Taylor Howard invented this device in 1976.

First DVDs
Several companies combined to produce these for the first time in 1995.

MOST POPULAR
Video Games

Platforms come and go, but some games stay on top no matter what console you play them on. Super Mario Brothers just seems to be super popular. So does Pokémon, in every color. This list is the top 15 games in sales through the middle of 2006. It covers all the games created since 1995.

GAME/PLATFORM	SALES (IN MILLIONS OF GAMES)
Super Mario Bros./NES[1]	40.24
Pokémon Red, Blue, and Green/GB[2]	31.37
Tetris/GB	30.26
Duck Hunt/NES	28.31
Pokémon Gold and Silver/GBC[3]	23.10
Super Mario World/SNES[4]	20.61
Super Mario Land/GB	18.14
Super Mario Bros. 3/NES	18.00
Pokémon Ruby and Sapphire/GBA[5]	14.74
Pokémon Yellow/GB	14.64
Gran Turismo 3: A-Spec/PS2[6]	14.36
Grand Theft Auto: Vice City/PS2	13.58
Grand Theft Auto: San Andreas/PS2	13.47
Super Mario 64/N64[7]	11.89
Grand Theft Auto III/PS2	11.39

[1]Nintendo Entertainment System, [2]Nintendo Game Boy, [3]Game Boy Color, [4]Super Nintendo Entertainment System, [5]Nintendo Game Boy Advance, [6]Sony PlayStation 2, [7]Nintendo 64

Pop Culture
Game Page

Okay, we need your help. There's been a massive computer glitch at a gigantic pop culture Web site. Dozens of superstars' names have been mixed up in horrible ways. You need to unscramble the names below (all found in this chapter) and then take the first letters of the resulting names and put them, in order, in the blanks at the bottom to form the mystery word at the bottom (the source of the computer bug, as it turns out).

NENJFEIR NTNAISO   _____ _____

EIC EUCB   _____ _____

RAIMO SHOBTRER   _____ _____

EXLLWAM ASRTM   _____ _____

EIELLNV OOOGLMNBTT   _____ _____

IVELS ELESRPY   _____ _____

HRUSE   _____

IIKT ERRBAB   _____ _____

PLARH GUMGIW   _____ _____

HAORP WRIENYF   _____ _____

MNEO   _____

Answer: __ __ __ __ Y   __ __ __ __ __

CHAPTER SEVEN

Animals

Sure, we've got some of the "usual" animals in here, like dogs (ugly ones) and horses (including some from Xilingol). But we've also got poisonous lizards, bugs the size of your hand, and waterskiing squirrels.
Be an animal . . . and dig in!

Champion Dogs

The Westminster Kennel Club Dog Show is the oldest and most famous dog show in the United States. The annual winner of Best in Show is considered America's top dog! In the years since the first Westminster show in 1877, here are the breeds that have won the most Bests in Show.

BREED/NO. OF BEST IN SHOW WINNERS

Wire Fox Terrier/13

Scottish Terrier/7

English Springer Spaniel/5

Airedale Terrier/4

Pekingese/3

Pointer/3

Miniature Poodle/3

Name That Dog!

Your average, everyday dog can get by with a name like Spot or Sam or Fifi. But dog-show dogs need really big dog tags to fit their names. Take the 2006 Westminster winner. He was a Bull Terrier named (deep breath) Ch. [for "Champion"] Rocky Top's Sundance Kid. To make it easy, he also answers to "Rufus."

Ugly Dog WINNERS

Not every dog is a cute and cuddly puppy. Some of them are downright ugly. Ugly, that is, to everyone but their loving owners. All in the spirit of fun, numerous "ugly dog" contests are held around the country. Here are stories about some of the winners.

Sam, a nearly hairless Chinese Crested with crooked teeth and wrinkly skin, was the most famous "ugly dog" in the world until his death at age 14 in 2005. He won contests around the world and appeared on numerous TV shows.

Hoss was the three-time winner of a contest in North Carolina. He was a mix of Labrador Retriever and Basset Hound, but what made him, well, unique was an "an underbite that makes his bottom teeth stick out like a barracuda," according to one newspaper.

Sushi, a Japanese Chin mix, won a radio station contest in Medford, Massachusetts. Her wrinkly brown skin, mismatched eyes, and blunt snout wowed (or grossed out) the judges.

Zippy was another Chinese Crested who had a habit of sticking her tongue out the side of her mouth. She won a pile of ugly dog contests and was featured on TV, in books, and on calendars.

MOST POPULAR
Pet Names

See Spot run. See Spot sit. See Spot complain that his name is too boring and that he wants a new one! Here's a list of some alternatives for naming your dog or cat. These are the most popular names, based on how often the name has been put on a pet tag.

Max	Sadie
Jake	Lucky
Buddy	Rocky
Maggie	Lucy
Bear	Daisy
Molly	Buster
Bailey	Casey
Shadow	Cody
Sam	Brandy
Lady	Duke

Unusual Pets

There are about 60 million pet dogs in the United States and about 70 million pet cats. And don't forget about a gazillion pet fish. But those are everyday pets, pets everyone has seen or, well, petted (except maybe the fish). Here's a list of real animals that some people (okay, maybe just a few people) keep as pets. Ask your mom and dad to check these out!

African giant millipedes

African pygmy hedgehogs

Chinchillas

Ferrets

Hermit crabs

Madagascar hissing cockroaches

Potbellied pigs

Prairie dogs

Stick insects

Tarantulas

Tree frogs

Exotic Tips

Pets like these are known as "exotic" pets, and they need some special care. Here are a few random tips about living with some of these animals: • Ferrets can be litter-box-trained like cats. • You have to trim the tusks of potbellied pigs. • Don't pick a hedgehog up from the top. • Hissing cockroaches eat crushed dry dog or cat food; put Vaseline on the edge of an aquarium so they can't get out.

ANIMALS

Presidential Pets

Just because the president of the United States has to move into the White House doesn't mean he can't take his pets with him. Since George Washington brought a parrot with him when he took the job, most presidents have enjoyed the company of something four-legged, feathered, or furry. Until the 20th century, they all had horses, and of course, there were dogs and cats aplenty. Here's a list of some of the more interesting and the more recent First Animals.

PRESIDENT	PETS
Thomas Jefferson	pair of brown bear cubs
John Quincy Adams	alligator
Abraham Lincoln	turkey named Jack, two goats
James A. Garfield	dog named Veto*
Benjamin Harrison	opossum
Theodore Roosevelt	macaw, guinea pig, flying squirrel, raccoon, owl, hyena, and zebra, among many others
Woodrow Wilson	ram named Old Ike
Calvin Coolidge	bobcat, bear, pygmy hippo, and Enoch the goose, among others
Franklin D. Roosevelt	a Scottish Terrier named Fala
John F. Kennedy	ponies, horses, parakeets, and many dogs
Lyndon Johnson	beagles named Him and Her
George H. W. Bush	Springer Spaniel named Millie#
William Jefferson Clinton	Socks the cat and Buddy the Labrador Retriever
George W. Bush	dogs named Spot and Barney, cat named India

*That's a presidential joke; when a president gives his veto, he refuses to sign a bill into law.

#In 1990, Millie "wrote" a bestselling book about life in the White House.

Animals with
Horns

First, a definition: Horns are permanent, bony parts of animals. Antlers, unlike bones, can have forks, or different branches, and they are shed annually. Horns are usually on an animal for life. This list includes animal families — all mammals — from around the world that have horns, and, of course, this means they have a tough time putting sweaters on over their heads. Just kidding . . . this means they have horns that they use in self-defense, as a way to attract mates, or as tools to find food. Don't let anybody horn in on you while you're reading this list!

Antelope
Bison
Cow
Deer
Giraffe
Goat
Narwhal
Rhinoceros
Sheep

Cool fact: Rhinoceros horns are not made of bone, but of tightly compacted hair! Sadly, many rhinos have been killed by poachers who want only the horns, which are sold as souvenirs or as "magic" powder.

Apes & Monkeys

Apes and monkeys are our closest relatives in the animal kingdom, but they can be sort of confusing. How do you tell the difference between the two? These lists sort out the species. Then we'll explain a few ways you can tell if an animal is a monkey, an ape, or your little brother or sister.

TYPES OF APES

Bonobo

Chimpanzee

Gibbon

Gorilla

Orangutan

Siamang

TYPES OF MONKEYS

Baboon

Capuchin

Celebes

Colobus

Guenon

Howler

Langur

Macaque

Mandrill

Mangabey

Marmoset

Proboscis

Rhesus

Sake

TYPES OF MONKEYS, CONTINUED

Spider
Squirrel
Tamarin
Titi
Uakari
Woolly

Ape or Monkey:
What's the Difference?

Apes and monkeys (and humans, too!) are all primates. All have hair, eyes that face front, opposable thumbs, and fingernails instead of claws. But there are some differences. Here's a handy list:

APES	MONKEYS
✔ No tails	✔ Most have tails
✔ Can reach up to grab branches	✔ Can't reach up
✔ Can walk on two feet	✔ Walk only on four feet
✔ May have bare patches on face	✔ Hair all over face
✔ Larger brain	✔ Smaller brain
✔ Have learned sign language	✔ Haven't learned sign language

Accidental Tourists

Animals are usually native to one place. A particular species has a geographic range in which it is most comfortable. Sort of like how you feel at home in your neighborhood, but would be out of place if you moved to, say, Mongolia (unless your neighborhood is in Mongolia). However, some animals travel to new homes by accident. They stick to ships, are blown off course by winds, or are brought in by people. Then they become "invasive" species, often doing harm to native wildlife or plants. Here is a list of such species in the United States.

- Africanized honeybee
- Asian long-horned beetle
- Brown tree snake
- Cactus moth
- Cane toad
- European gypsy moth
- European starling
- Flathead catfish
- Formosan subterranean termite
- Glassy-winged sharpshooter
- Green crab
- Hibiscus mealybug
- Red imported fire ant
- Rosy wolfsnail
- Russian wheat aphid
- Silverleaf whitefly
- Wild boar
- Zebra mussel

Pandas
with Passports

As you probably know, the giant panda is native to China. That's the only place in the world where these shy and rare animals live in the wild. However, so many people around the world want to see pandas up close that China loans some of the animals to zoos around the world. As of 2006, these are the giant pandas living outside of China.

PANDAS/ZOO SITE

Lun Lun, Yang Yang, Mei Lan/Atlanta, Ga.

Bao Bao, Yan Yan/Berlin, Germany

Tan Tan, Kou Kou/Kobe, Japan

Ling Ling/Kyoto, Japan

Ya Ya, La La/Memphis, Tenn.

Xiu Hua, Shuang Shuang, Xin Xin/Mexico City, Mexico

Bai Yun, Gao Gao, Su Lin, Mei Sheng/San Diego, Calif.

Mei Mei, Lau Hin/Wakayama, Japan

Mei Xiang, Tian Tian/Washington, D.C.

Note: There may be a giant panda in a zoo in North Korea, but no one knows for sure because that country is mostly closed to visitors.

Big Birds!

Most birds are rather small, usually cute, and tweet a lot. That's not what this list is about, however. This list is about the biggest members of the bird family. These are not songbirds for your backyard feeder; these are the elephants of birdland. (Note: The tall, yellow bird from that popular TV show is not on our list!) Their homes are listed with their names.

Biggest Bird
The ostrich (Africa) is the tallest and heaviest bird. They can weigh about 250-300 lbs. (113-136 kg) and stand 8-9 ft. (2.4-2.7 m) tall. They also lay the largest eggs in the bird world; one ostrich egg would hold 24 chicken eggs! However, ostriches can't fly.

Largest Flying Bird
The Kori bustard (Africa) and the great bustard (Europe) somehow get aloft even though they weigh about 40 lbs. (18.1 kg).

Tallest Flying Birds
Some species of cranes, which live in many places around the world, can be as much as 6 ft., 6 in. (2 m) tall.

Widest Wingspan
The mighty albatross (Southern Hemisphere) has wings that measure – from tip to tip while fully spread – as much as 11 ft. (3.3 m).

Biggest Bill
Only birds (and duckbilled platypuses, of course) have bills. The longest bills in the bird world belong to Australian pelicans, whose bills can be up to 18 in. (46 cm) long.

 Okay, once and for all: Do ostriches really stick their heads in the sand? You've probably seen them do it in cartoons, but in real life, they are just putting their heads near the ground to fool far-off predators into thinking that the bushy bird is, well, a bush.

ANIMALS

WORLD'S
Rarest Birds

Ornithologists (people who study birds) were thrilled in 2004 when reports came out of Louisiana that an ivory-billed woodpecker had been spotted in a swamp. The bird had not been seen in the wild since 1944 and was believed to be extinct. Here is a list of other extremely rare birds. The population of each of these birds is estimated to be less than 250!

BIRD	MAIN RANGE
Alagoas curassow	Brazil
Bishop's 'o'o	Hawaii
Black-breasted puffin	Ecuador
California condor	California
Chinese crested tern	Asia
Crested ibis	China
Zino's petrel	Madeira
Giant ibis	Cambodia
Gurney's pitta	Malaysia
Imperial Amazon parrot	Dominica
Ivory-billed woodpecker	Louisiana
Jerdon's courser	India
Junin grebe	Peru
Kinglet cotinga	Brazil
Madagascar serpent-eagle	Madagascar
Mauritius parakeet	Mauritius
Rapa fruit-dove	Tahiti
Seychelles magpie-robin	Seychelles
Slender-billed curlew	Russia
Polynesian ground-dove	Moorea
Socorro mockingbird	Mexico
Spix's macaw	Brazil
White-eyed river-martin	Thailand
Yellow-eared parrot	Colombia

Really, Really
Poisonous Snakes

First of all, snakes are not slimy. Also, most of them are perfectly harmless to humans. But a list of all the harmless snakes would be boring. This list features some of the most poisonous snakes in the world. Just a few drops of their venom can take down a person or a large animal. We've also included a handy list of their homes . . . so you can stay away from them!

SNAKE	WHERE TO AVOID THEM
Australian brown snake	Australia
Beaked sea snake	Southeast Asia
Black mamba	South America
Boomslang	Africa
Brazilian huntsman	Brazil
Bushmaster	North America
Coral snake	North America
Death adder	Australia, Papua New Guinea
Gabon viper	Africa
Indian cobra	India
Inland taipan	Australia
Malayan krait	Indonesia, Southeast Asia
Mojave rattlesnake	North America
Saw-scaled viper	Middle East, North Africa
Tiger snake	Australia

The Gila monster and Mexican beaded lizard are the only poisonous lizards in the world. They live in the southwestern United States and northern Mexico. Please don't step on them.

Big Bugs!

Bugs are not something that you want to be big. Big snacks? Sure. Big pieces of cake? Definitely. Your favorite sports team's score? Of course. But bugs? No . . . you'd probably rather they were small and scarce. However, some insects are just plain big. This is a list of some things that you really hope do not land on your head. (Their homes are listed with their names.)

Heaviest Insect

While not too big compared to, say, a dog, compared to an ant, the goliath beetle (Africa) is a giant! The biggest ones can be almost as big as a tennis ball and weigh a quarter-pound (100 g).

Longest Insect

The well-named stick insect (Indonesia) can be more than a foot (30 cm) long.

Biggest Moth

The Atlas moth (Asia) has a wingspan of 10–11 in. (25–28 cm), about as big across as your two hands spread out.

Farthest Jumping Insect

The froghopper, or spittlebug, which lives all over the world, can leap up to 28 in. (71 cm), which is 115 times its body length. If you could jump like one, you'd be able to jump to the top of the Washington Monument.

Biggest Spider

Yes, we know spiders are not insects. They're arachnids. The biggest spider in the world lives in South America. The goliath bird-eating spider is only scary if you're a bird, but it is really huge and can measure 11 in. (28 cm) across!

ONLY IN
Australia

As an island continent cut off for centuries by vast oceans, Australia is the home of some of the world's most unique animals. With little contact with the wider world, these animals developed over time into some of the world's most unusual species. There are hundreds of Australia-only snakes, lizards, and insects, but this list is just Aussie mammals. Although these animals are now seen in zoos around the world, Australia remains the only place they call home.

Dingo This is the wild dog of the Australian Outback.

Kangaroo Several species of this large marsupial are found in Australia; they are best known for their large hind legs and jumping ability, and for carrying their young in a pouch.

Koala Another marsupial, this shy tree-dwelling mammal is cute, fuzzy, and eats only eucalyptus leaves.

Platypus This is the only mammal that lays eggs and has a bird-like bill, plus has a flat tail like a beaver.

Quokka These small marsupials look a bit like large rats with short noses.

Tasmanian devil These small and fierce creatures are the last meat-eating marsupials left in the world.

Wombat Wombats come in several species, but most are small, burrowing, nocturnal animals. The northern hairy-nosed wombat is one of the rarest animals in the world.

Kids' Favorite
Types of Fish

Everyone knows that fish is good for you to eat. It supplies many important nutrients, along with being a good source of protein for energy. So this list is filled with examples of the many foods from the sea that kids love. See if your favorite is on this list.

Tuna

Animals
At Work

For thousands of years, animals and humans have worked side by side on farms around the world. Horses carry riders, cows and oxen pull plows, sheep cut grass and share their wool, and chickens lay eggs. But away from the farmyard and the field, animals are hard at work doing other jobs. Here's a list of animals that deserve to earn a paycheck — if only they had pockets to keep their wallets in.

Bloodhounds

These dogs use their supersensitive noses to help track down missing people.

Guide dogs

They assist blind people by helping them get around safely.

Guard geese

At some military installations, geese patrol to help alert the guards to the presence of strangers.

Helper monkeys

Capuchin monkeys work as personal helpers for people in wheelchairs and people with disabilities.

Lab rats
Rats and mice are often used in scientific experiments.

Lumberjack elephants
In India and Thailand, elephants are trained to work with riders to lift heavy logs.

Minesweeper dolphins
Specially trained dolphins help navies search for undersea mines.

Medical maggots
It's kind of gross, but maggots (fly larvae) can be used by doctors to help clean wounds. And yes, they eat the dead flesh!

Police dogs
Working with specially trained officers, K-9 dogs are used to help chase down suspects or to help search for missing people. Other dogs are trained to sniff for explosives or illegal substances.

Truffle pigs
Trained pigs search for valuable truffles, a type of underground fungus somewhat like a mushroom.

Horsin' Around

Among the dozens and dozens of horse breeds from around the world, there is at least one that starts with every letter of the alphabet. Perhaps the most popular breeds are the American Quarter Horse, the American Paint Horse, the Arabian, the Thoroughbred, and the Appaloosa. On this trip through the equine (that means having to do with horses) alphabet, how many have you heard of?

Andalusian	**N**orwegian fjörd
Budyonny	**O**b
Camargue	**P**alomino
Dartmoor pony	**Q**uarab
Egyptian	**R**acking horse
Florida cracker	**S**hetland pony
Guangxi	**T**ennessee walking horse
Hanoverian	**U**kranian saddle horse
Icelandic	**V**laamperd
Jutland	**W**elsh pony
Kisber felver	**X**ilingol
Lipizzan	**Y**akut
Mustang	**Z**aniskari pony

Best Zoos
for You

Zoos are awesome places to visit. You can see interesting animals up close (and they can see you — did you ever think about that?). You can learn more about their habitats and habits. And you can bug your parents to buy you a souvenir. *Child* magazine did a survey that looked at all the zoos in the United States. They chose these 10 as the best "family-friendly" zoos. Next time you're near one, stop by and let the animals say hi to you.

RANK ZOO/CITY

1 **Lowry Park Zoo/**Tampa, Fla.

2 **San Diego Zoo/**San Diego, Calif.

3 **Oklahoma City Zoological Park and Botanical Garden/**Oklahoma City, Okla.

4 **Brookfield Zoo/**Brookfield, Ill.

5 **Phoenix Zoo/**Phoenix, Ariz.

6 **Cincinnati Zoo and Botanical Garden/**Cincinnati, Ohio

7 **Bronx Zoo/**New York, N.Y.

8 **Toledo Zoo/**Toledo, Ohio

9 **Fort Wayne Children's Zoo/**Fort Wayne, Ind.

10 **Columbus Zoo & Aquarium/**Columbus, Ohio

Zoo Food

Your parents have it tough. They have to work hard to buy the good food that keeps you healthy — and they usually have to make it for you, too. But you're just kids — imagine if they had to feed an entire zoo! The kitchen folks at zoos around the country have to do that every day. For instance, the nine chimps at Miami's Metrozoo eat 7,000 oranges a year, cut into 26,280 pieces! Miami's 175 fruit bats enjoy 270 gallons of peach nectar a year! For a more complete picture, the animal chefs (chefs for animals, that is, not animals as chefs!) at the St. Louis Zoo provided this inside peek at a full year's menu to feed everything from aardvarks to zebras. Their Animal Nutrition Center staff uses this food and more to feed the hundreds of animals at their zoo. Dig in!

120 pounds (54.5 kg) of earthworms

313 cases of kale

1.4 tons of spinach

1.5 tons of squid

6 tons of monkey biscuits

7.5 tons of smelt

10 tons of dog food
(for various animals, not for dogs!)

10 tons of mackerel

13 tons of bananas

21 tons of apples

22 tons of carrots

72 tons of pellets for herbivores
(plant-eaters)

PLUS

6,000 waxworms

8,900 adult mice

10,000 bales of hay

52,000 super mealworms

260,000 flightless houseflies

625,000 mealworms

1.5 million crickets

It Takes a Village to Raise a Panda

Lun Lun, a panda at the Atlanta Zoo and a new mom (see page 207), and her "husband" Yang Yang have a lot of help raising her new cub. A trio of keepers spends 70 hours a week just taking care of Yang Yang. Five other keepers, including a panda expert brought in from China, care for Lun Lun and the cub round-the-clock. Four people chop 1,250 pounds (567 kg) of bamboo every week to feed the pandas. That's a lot of "panda pals"!

Amazing Animals

Your dog can do a trick or two, probably. He can sit or roll over or fetch. Maybe you've trained your cat to play with a toy. Big deal! After you read about these real-life animal feats, you'll look at your own pets in a whole new way!

Agatha
Though blind, this "watch cat" attacked and chased away a burglar trying to break into her owner's house.

Buster
A Springer Spaniel and a member of Great Britain's Royal Army, Buster is trained to sniff out explosives. He located a huge pile of weapons in Iraq and received a special award.

Brutus
This Dachshund is a dog with no fear. He goes skydiving with his owner, Ron Sirull.

Mkombozi
A stray dog in Kenya, Mkombozi (the name, which the dog got later, means "savior") found an abandoned human baby and kept her alive for several days until rescuers found the girl.

Reno
This police dog in Des Moines, Iowa, won an award for helping save two fellow officers, even after he was wounded by a criminal suspect.

Tommy
When his owner fell and could not get up, this dog used speed-dial on a phone to call 911 and get help.

Ueno
This faithful Akita dog continued to go to a train station daily to meet his owner – for 10 years after the owner died! A statue in Japan honors this loyal pooch.

Twiggy
A squirrel who waterskis. Seriously!

All the Way Back

The Endangered Species Act is a law that gives special protection to animal (and plant) species that are being threatened with extinction for a variety of reasons. Species are added to the list when their numbers drop dangerously low, but the good news is that, thanks to the efforts of many people, some animals have come off the list. This means their numbers have increased enough that their survival is no longer in question. Here are the animals that have been removed from the U.S. Fish & Wildlife Threatened and Endangered Species System lists:

ANIMAL	PUT ON LIST	TAKEN OFF LIST
Aleutian Canada goose	1967	2001
American alligator	1967	1987
American peregrine falcon	1970	1999
Brown pelican	1967	1985
Columbian white-tailed deer	1967	2004*
Gray whale	1970	1994**
Grizzly bear	1975	2005
Palau fantailed flycatcher	1970	1985
Palau ground dove	1970	1985
Palau owl	1970	1985
Tinian monarch bird	1970	2004

*Oregon only   **Eastern North Pacific Ocean only

Dolphin OR Porpoise?

A marine mammal swims up to you and you want to say hi. But you don't want to embarrass yourself and it by calling it a dolphin if it's a porpoise, or a porpoise if it's a dolphin. So how do you tell the difference? Well, we're here to help with this handy clip-and-save (but not if it's a library book!) chart about these two related but different aquatic creatures. Why does this matter? Well, it would matter more if you were a dolphin or a porpoise, right?

Dolphin	Porpoise
Smaller head	Bigger head
Longer snout	Shorter snout
Larger bodies	(Usually) smaller bodies
Cone-shaped teeth	Flat, triangular teeth
Dorsal (back) fin can be curved on one edge	Fins are triangular

Bonus Confusion!

As if that wasn't confusing enough, there is a fish that goes by many names, one of which is — get this — "dolphin fish"! Its other names include dorado and mahi-mahi. So if you see "dolphin" on the menu at a seafood restaurant, it's this fish, not the friendly mammal of the same name.

The Dish on Fish

Tropical fish swimming around a pleasant aquarium can be a beautiful and calming addition to any home or classroom. There are literally hundreds of types of fish — saltwater and freshwater — that people keep as pets. Here is a list of some of the most popular (note that there are dozens of different types of some of these species).

FRESHWATER FISH

Angelfish

Betta

Cichlid

Discus

Goldfish

Gourami

Guppy

Loach

Oscar

Tetra

SALTWATER FISH

Angelfish

Clown fish

Goby

Lionfish

Wrasse

Yellow tang

Animals
Game Page

You've heard of the "circle of life," right? That's the deal where big animals eat small animals, then the big animals die and become part of the ground, and the plants grow in the ground, and the little animals eat the plants, then the big animals come along and do it all over again. Well, we've got our own little circle of life right here. Starting with the number 1 and moving clockwise, fill in the blanks. The first letter of each word will be the last letter of the word in front of it. Take the letters in the shaded circles and unscramble them to find the mystery words at the bottom, describing a popular type of animal.

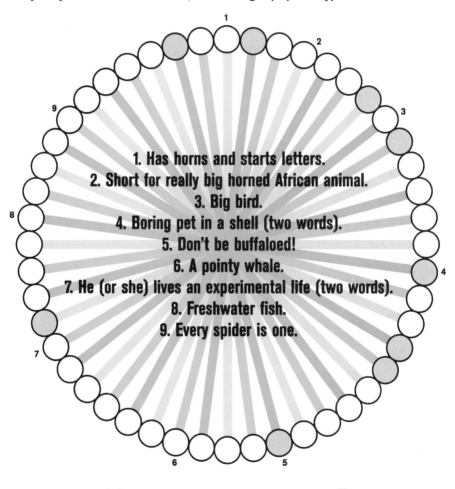

1. Has horns and starts letters.
2. Short for really big horned African animal.
3. Big bird.
4. Boring pet in a shell (two words).
5. Don't be buffaloed!
6. A pointy whale.
7. He (or she) lives an experimental life (two words).
8. Freshwater fish.
9. Every spider is one.

_ U _ _ _   _ _ _ _ _ G _

CHAPTER EIGHT

Food

While reading this chapter, feel free to wipe your mouth on your sleeve, read with your elbows on the table, and eat with your hands. Just don't get food on the book! *Bon appétit!*

MORE Gross Stuff

In the first edition of the *Scholastic Book of Lists*, we learned that people eat a heck of a lot of strange stuff. Sheep eyeballs in India, tarantula kebabs in Cambodia, toasted termites in South Africa, and many other unappetizing foods. Well, we didn't want to stop there. We scoured the world and found more really gross things that people actually eat. Put on a napkin (or get a bucket handy) and dig in to this list.

FOOD	WHERE THEY EAT IT
Alligator-on-a-stick	**United States**
Bats	**Indonesia**
Camel's feet	**France**
Cow's blood	**Africa**

Some cattle-herding tribes drink it straight from the cow.

Cow brain tacos	**Mexico**
Fish head soup	**China**
Fugu	**Japan**

A type of blowfish; if not prepared just right, it is very poisonous!

Fish eyes	**Asia**
Haggis	**Scotland**

It's the stomach of a sheep, stuffed with all the rest of its organs and roasted with oats and herbs.

Jellied eels	**England**

People Really Eat

Purple seaweed	**Canada**
Salamanders	**Japan**
Squirrel brains	**United States**
Surströmming	**Sweden**

It's a herring dish left out for months, so that it ends up being really, really stinky.

Turducken	**United States**

A turkey stuffed with a duck that has been stuffed with a chicken.

Yak butter	**India, Tibet**

Gross Candy

Want to eat a booger? A piece of roadkill? Some earwax? Well, you can . . . and live to tell about it. That's because lots of candymakers are using your love of gross things to make candies with yucky flavors. There are jelly beans that taste like boogers and candy shaped like squashed possums. You can eat candy dispensed from the, um, wrong end of a pig, or candy designed to look like brain drippings!

Strange Soda

Bubbly, sugary, flavored soda (or pop, depending on where you live) is one of America's most popular drinks. Most flavors are pretty standard: cola, lemon-lime, orange, and so on. One company, Jones Soda Co. of Washington, is different. They have created a variety of soda flavors that you won't find at your local fast-food place. Check out their list of very unusual soda flavors, most made specially for Thanksgiving.

Brussels sprouts soda

Cranberry soda

Fruitcake soda

Green bean casserole soda

Mashed potato soda

Pumpkin pie soda

Turkey and gravy soda

Wild herb stuffing soda

Too busy to make a big Thanksgiving dinner? The Jones Soda Company sells its Turkey Day sodas in a special pack so that you can drink your whole meal. They've also made one-time batches of ham- and fish-taco-flavored sodas. The cool thing is that the money they make from these is used to benefit charities like Toys for Tots!

Weird Ice Cream

Chocolate. Strawberry. Mint chip. The old standby — vanilla. Those are the ice-cream flavors we're used to. The tried and true. The traditional. Booorrrrring! On this page, we expand our ice-cream universe and feature those flavors that go beyond the everyday, outside of the normal, and into the truly and icily odd. Many of these are only sold in Japan, but some can be found by adventurous eaters in other places. Dig in!

Fish

Guacamole
(avocado)

Lobster

Minestrone

Octopus

Pickle

Praline-chili

Salmon

Sauerkraut

Sea slug

Shrimp

Sweet potato

Whale

Poisonous Ice Cream?

One of the world leaders in bizarre ice-cream flavors is Japanese ice-cream maven Yoshiaki Sato. His shop — called Fugetsudo in Ishinomaki, Japan — has made more than 80 unusual flavors. One of the hardest to make was pit viper. Mr. Sato had to put the poisonous (but skinned and steamed) snake in a blender (yuck!), then mush it together with ice-cream fixings like sugar and cream. Small towns in Japan hire him to make fish flavors for local fairs and parties.

Champion Eaters

Don't read this list if you're hungry . . . or if you've just finished a big meal. Seriously. This list celebrates world-champion eaters, people who can shovel away an enormous amount of food in a pretty short amount of time. This "hobby" has gotten so popular that the International Federation of Competitive Eating was formed to help keep track of all the pounds, gallons, and feet of food going down. Looking over their long list of records, here are some of the most amazing. Oh, and please . . . don't try these at home (or school!).

FOOD	TIME	EATER	AMOUNT
Baked beans	1:48	Don Leman	6 lbs. (2.72 kg)
Chicken nuggets	5:00	Sonya Thomas	80 nuggets
Chili	10:00	Richard LeFevre	1.5 gal. (5.68 l)
Cow brains	15:00	Takeru Kobayashi	17.7 lbs. (8.03 kg)
Donuts	8:00	Eric Booker	49 donuts
French fries	6:00	Cookie Jarvis	4.46 lbs. (2.02 kg)
Hot dogs (with buns)	12:00	Takeru Kobayashi	53.5 hot dogs
Mayonnaise	8:00	Oleg Zhomitskiy	128 oz. (3.78 l)
Onions	1:00	Eric Booker	3 @ 8.5 oz. (241 g) ea.
Pizza	15:00	Richard LeFevre	7.5 slices
Quesadillas	5:00	Sonya Thomas	31.4 4-in. (10-cm) quesadillas

? Takeru Kobayashi is perhaps the world's most famous speed-eater. He has won the Nathan's Famous Hot Dog Eating Contest on New York's Coney Island for six years running. What's amazing about him is that he's very normal-sized; he weighs only 160 pounds (72 kg). One of his competitors in 2006 weighed 425 pounds (193 kg)!

Sushi Names

Sushi is a Japanese way of preparing seafood. Specially trained chefs put together an amazing assortment of fish, shellfish, and seaweed with rice and other ingredients. The results are colorful and tasty . . . but often raw! That's right, many types of sushi are raw fish. Don't be chicken . . . try some raw fish. Here are some of the words you'll see on sushi menus.

SUSHI	WHAT IS IT?
Nigiri sushi	Bite-sized portions of rice topped with different kinds of raw or cooked fish.
Gunkan sushi	A sort of cup made of dried seaweed and filled with rice and fish.
Maki sushi	Larger pieces of dried seaweed are covered with rice, fish, and vegetables, and then rolled. The roll is then cut into pieces. The California roll, which contains crab, avocado, and cucumber, is the most well-known type.

Sushi ingredients

Anago	**Eel**
Ebi	**Shrimp**
Hamachi	**Yellowtail** (a kind of tuna)
Ikura	**Cooked chicken eggs**
Maguro	**Tuna**
Uni	**Sea urchin eggs**
Wasabi	**A super-hot Japanese horseradish**

Edible Flowers

Roses are pretty, but are they tasty? Nasturtiums spread their vines everywhere; what would they taste like spreading around in your mouth? You eats lots of fruits and vegetables (don't you?), so why not flowers? Here is a list of some of the many flowers that are usually safe to eat. However, before you jump into your neighbor's garden with a knife and fork, ask your parents. Flowers for eating should not have been sprayed with any pesticides or chemicals.

Bachelor's button
(petals only)

Chamomile
(also makes a lovely tea)

Chrysanthemum

Dandelion

Elderberry

Geranium

Hibiscus

Honeysuckle

Lavender

Lilac

Marigold

Mint

Nasturtium

Snapdragon

Violet
(can be candy-coated!)

Um, "bachelor's buttons"? The puffy, often blue flowers resemble, apparently, a type of collar button or cuff link that men used to wear.

Edible Insects

Of course, *edible* (meaning something that can be eaten) and *insects* are not two words you usually expect to go together. Disgusting insects, maybe, nasty insects . . . but *edible*? Well, surprise! Insects are eaten all over the world, as snacks, main dishes, condiments, and desserts. One survey we found counted more than 1,400 types of insects that can be eaten. The good news is that most insects are very low in fat. Here are a few of the more popular types of edible (for someone else!) insects.

INSECT/HOW THEY ARE PREPARED

Ants/Fried, chocolate-covered

Ant eggs/Raw

Cockroaches/Fried, steamed

Crickets/Fried

Silkworm grubs/Steamed, fried

Caterpillars/Raw, fried

Grasshoppers/
Fried, steamed

Mealworms/
Fried, sautéed

Hu-hu grubs/Raw

Scorpion/Fried,
boiled

Tarantulas/Fried

Termites/Fried

Water bugs/
Steamed, boiled

Witchety grubs*/
Various

*Inspired by Aboriginal cuisine, many Australians have tried this traditional native food.

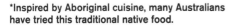

Famous Feasts

Huge feasts have been held throughout history, to celebrate a big event or just to show off how much food a king has. Other dining events are just, well, weird. As you get ready to eat . . . er, read this list of famous feasts, tuck in your napkin, pick up your fork, and dig in.

Fit for a King (or 50)

In her very cool book *Charlemagne's Feast*, author Nochola Fletcher lists the "41,833 items of meat and poultry," including rabbits, pigs, oxen, deer, and 18 different kinds of birds, served at a 1465 feast to celebrate a new bishop in York, England.

A Mess of Mayors

In 1900, 22,295 mayors from French towns ate together on tables that were so big that some of the 3,600 waiters used bikes. The mayors downed 15,000 lbs. (6,803 kg) of pheasant, salmon, and other fowl, accompanied by 50,000 bottles of wine.

Wonder What the Horses Ate

In 1903, millionaire horseman C. K. Billings hosted a dinner for 30 of his pals, but the hook was that they had to eat on horseback. Billings rented and renovated a ballroom to fit all the mounts and their eating riders.

Diamond Dining

Railroad tycoon "Diamond" Jim Brady was one of history's great eaters. Legend has it that his typical meal included three dozen oysters, six lobsters, a steak, two ducks, piles of vegetables, and soup. He didn't drink wine, so he glugged a gallon or so of orange juice. In 1905, he gave an enormous banquet honoring his racehorse.

A Bridge to Indigestion

The *Guinness World Records* book lists the world's longest table, a 3-mile (5.05 km) table set up in 1998 across a bridge in Portugal. Fifteen thousand people sat down to eat at once.

Meals in Space

How do you eat when you're flying through space? Well, pizza delivery is out, of course (though space pizza delivery person would be a cool job). And with those bulky spacesuit gloves, it's hard to hold a sandwich. Plus, that whole zero-gravity thing means that food is floating around. The folks who send the space shuttles into orbit have figured out how to let astronauts eat well and stay healthy even in zero gravity. Here is a list of space food facts.

★ Each astronaut gets three meals a day, plus some snacks.

★ The space shuttle pantry can carry as many as 70 different food items and 20 beverages.

★ Drinks include coffee, tea, orange juice, and lemonade.

★ Drinks are packaged in pouches similar to juice boxes (so the liquids won't float away).

★ Some of the food choices include macaroni and cheese, spaghetti, chicken, beef, and lots of different kinds of fish.

★ What about salt and pepper? They have it, but it's in liquid form. You can imagine what a puff of pepper floating around could do to astronauts' eyes and noses!

★ No refrigerators on the space shuttle, so the food is often freeze-dried; that is, the water is removed from it. To eat something like mac and cheese, the astronaut adds some water to the pouch, heats it (they do have an oven), and digs in. Well, puts a straw in, anyway.

★ What about the leftovers? Astronauts work hard, so they always clean their plates, er, pouches. All the trash is compacted and carried back to Earth for disposal. No littering in space!

Eating IN THE Army

Soldiers in the field can't stop off for fast food, and they might be miles away from their base when it's time to eat. That's why the well-prepared U.S. soldier never leaves home without an MRE. That stands for Meal, Ready to Eat. Packed in a thick plastic bag, an MRE has everything the hungry soldier needs for a healthy meal on the go. Some of the meals can be heated with a special chemical pouch. Plus, the packages have to be sturdy enough to survive a parachute drop of more than 1,200 feet (380 m). Here's a list of things found in one typical meal, plus a list of some of the MRE menu choices.

Typical MRE Contents

"Chicken with Salsa and Mexican Rice"
8-ounce (227 g) pouch of chicken in salsa
5-ounce (142 g) pack of Mexican-style rice
1 fruit/cereal bar
1 packet of crackers
Packets of salt, pepper, sugar, and jelly
Instant coffee
Chewing gum
Towelette
Plastic spoon
Matches
Toilet paper

Examples of MRE Varieties

Barbecued pork rib
Beef teriyaki
Black bean and rice burrito
Cajun rice with sausage
Cheese and vegetable omelet
Chicken fajita
Jambalaya
Manicotti with vegetables
Meat loaf with gravy
Turkey breast with gravy and potatoes

Good with Peanut Butter

Thanks to George Washington Carver, millions of kids don't go hungry at lunch. That's because the inventive peanut expert helped perfect that smooth or chunky stuff that we just couldn't live without. (Peanut butter was first sold at the St. Louis World's Fair in 1904 by cereal maker John Kellogg.) But peanut butter, as good as it is, is usually served with something else. Whether you put it on bread, crackers, bagels, apples, or celery, here are some of the most popular or unusual food items put together with P.B. (There's actually an entire store in New York City that sells almost nothing but peanut butter–based foods.)

Bacon
Bananas
Butter
Chocolate
Fried chicken
Honey

Jam
Jelly
Margarine
Marmalade
Marshmallows
Mayonnaise

Sandwich of "The King"

Elvis Presley was one of the most famous rock singers of all time and remains a legend to his fans. Almost as famous as his music was his odd taste in food. One item he enjoyed was a fried peanut butter and banana sandwich. Make sure and use white bread to get the full "King" treatment.

Food Firsts

The first meal of the day is breakfast. That's an easy one. Here are some other food firsts you can impress your friends with.

First Candy Canes

Sugar sticks bent into cane shapes were first seen in Germany in 1670; they were all white for many years before the familiar red stripe was added.

First Sandwich

John Montagu, the Earl of Sandwich in England, didn't want to leave his card game one day in 1762. He asked for meat and cheese between slices of bread — and the sandwich was born.

First Chewing Gum

In 1848, John Curtis invented State of Maine Pure Spruce Gum.

First Potato Chips

Oh, happy day! One evening in 1853 in Saratoga Springs, New York, chef George Crum was trying to please a picky eater. He tossed some thin slices of potato in boiling oil and ta-dah! The potato chip was born.

First Coca-Cola

The world's favorite soda was first made in 1886 by John Pemberton of Atlanta, Georgia.

First Girl Scout Cookies

Those tasty treats first went on sale in 1922.

First Popsicle

Frank Epperson accidentally left a glass of lemonade outdoors one night. It was frozen the next morning, and he realized he'd discovered something cool . . . literally! First sold as the Epsicle, it became the Popsicle in 1924.

First Drive-Through Restaurant

Leading to many happy future carpool stops, this pioneering eatery opened in Glendale, California, in 1926.

First Microwave Oven

This important kitchen tool isn't food, of course, but it changed the way we make food. The first microwave oven* was sold by the Raytheon Company in 1947. It was as big as a refrigerator!

First Big Mac

McDonald's most popular sandwich was first sold in 1968.

*Microwave ovens were actually discovered by accident when a scientist, Dr. Percy Spencer, was testing a magnetron tube and found that a chocolate bar in his pocket had melted!

Most kids would put pizza on their list of favorite foods. But kids in America's early years somehow managed to live without this essential food. The first pizzeria didn't open in the United States until 1895; it was Lombardi's in New York City.

School Lunch!

You probably eat lunch at school every day, unless you live close enough to go home for lunch . . . or you are homeschooled. Here's a question: If you would normally go home for lunch from school, do you go to school for lunch if you're homeschooled? Anyway, here are some fun facts about school lunches in the United States.

* The first free lunches in schools were served in 1853 in New York City.

* The National School Lunch program was started in 1946.

* By 1969, 19 million kids were enjoying tasty lunches (3.3 billion of them that year!). Those numbers rose to 29.6 million kids eating nearly 5 billion lunches by 2005.

* In 2005, 99,940,469 pints (47,289,479 l) of milk were gulped down through the Special Milk Program.

* Don't forget breakfast: The School Breakfast Program started in 1966.

* The second week of March is National School Breakfast Week.

* According to the U.S. Department of Agriculture, the top 10 breakfast food choices are:

Cold cereal	Pancakes
Toasted bread	Donuts
Biscuits	Waffles
Muffins	Hot cereal
Sweet rolls	Bagels/English muffins

* Some examples of school lunches from Philadelphia schools in the early 1900s: baked beans and roll; creamed beef on toast; macaroni with tomato sauce.

* Some examples from a 1940 cookbook for kids: egg and olive sandwich, corn muffin, and tomato; chicken leg, cheese-and-onion sandwich, fruit salad; cream of pea soup, egg-and-bacon sandwich, pears.

Food Chemicals

Have you ever tried to read the list of ingredients on the packaging of your favorite food? The words can be long and hard to pronounce; what do they mean? Using this list will help you understand what you are eating. By the way, ingredients are listed with the highest amount named first. So, if the first ingredient is fructose, your food item has lots of sugar in it!

THE FOOD:	YOU READ ON THE LABEL:	YOU'RE EATING:
candy, cookies, cakes, beverages, fruit snacks	corn syrup, fructose, glucose, sucrose, high fructose corn syrup	sugars: sweetens the food
candy, cheese, jelly, margarine, snack foods	annatto extract, beta-carotene, caramel color, carmine, cochineal extract, saffron	dyes: colors the food
beverages, luncheon meats, cereal, snack foods	ascorbic acid, BHA, BHT, calcium propionate, calcium nitrite, citric acid, potassium sorbate	preservatives: keeps food from spoiling
candy, cake, desserts, salad dressings, snack foods	carrageenan, cellulose gel, guar gum, modified food starch, olestra, whey protein concentrate	fat replacements: lowers fat content in food
cake, jelly, desserts, salad dressings, gelatin, pudding	carrageenan, gelatin, guar gum, whey, xanthan gum	thickeners: gives food specific textures
carbonated beverages, whipped cream	carbon dioxide, nitrous oxide	propellants: adds carbonation, aerates the food
bread, cereal, beverages, breakfast bars, flour	alpha tocopherols, amino acids, beta-carotene, iron sulfate, riboflavin, thiamine hydrochloride	vitamins/minerals: added back into food
bread, cakes, cookies	baking soda, calcium carbonate, monocalcium phosphate	leavening: helps food rise during baking

Famous Chefs

The most famous chef in your life, of course, is whoever in your house cooks the meals. But there are professional chefs out there who have become world famous for their way with food (and often, for their way-out personalities). Here's a short list of some of the most well-known names in the food biz.

Mario Batali New York–based chef who stars in several TV cooking shows.

Julia Child The late author and TV host made French cooking popular in America.

Bobby Flay Restaurant owner who became popular TV chef and cookbook author.

Emeril Lagasse Based in New Orleans, this TV chef is famous for saying "Bam!" when spicing food.

Nobu Matsuhisa He blends Japanese-style cooking with flavors of other nations.

Jamie Oliver His popular TV show was called *The Naked Chef*, but he wears clothes.

Wolfgang Puck A favorite of many movie stars, he turned pizza into a gourmet food.

Alice Waters Based in Berkeley, California, she promotes the use of fresh ingredients.

OCEAN FOOD THAT
Isn't Fish

You know all about tuna, but believe it or not, people eat other kinds of fish, too. There's more than one fish in the sea, as the old saying goes, and there's more than just fish, too. The ocean is home to hundreds of types of creatures who, through no fault of their own, are part of the world's diet. Here's a list of some animals from the sea that people enjoy eating.

Abalone	Oyster
Clam	Scallop
Conch	Sea cucumber
Crab	Shrimp
Lobster	Snail
Mussel	Squid
Octopus	

Another Kind of Chowder

You may have heard of clam chowder, but what about conch chowder? It's pronounced KONK, and is a popular dish in the Florida Keys and on Caribbean islands. In 1982, the city of Key West, Florida, declared itself an independent country (they were mostly joking) and renamed itself the Conch Republic.

Talking Food

Coming up with a list of food-related words was a piece of cake! We don't list them all here, of course, just the cream of the crop. These phrases have entered the English language hot out of the oven, ready to dress up sentences as well as dinner tables. If your favorite isn't in here, don't cry over spilled milk. You're still the apple of our eye.

apple of his/her eye
A person who is very much loved by another person

big cheese
The boss, an important person

bring home the bacon
Earn a living, support a household

butter up
Flatter or kiss up to someone

cool as a cucumber
Describing a person who is calm and confident in a tough situation

couch potato
A lazy person who watches too much TV — let's hope this isn't you!

don't cry over spilled milk
Don't make a fuss over small things or things you can't fix

egg on your face
Being embarrassed

half-baked
An idea that is incomplete or unworkable

hot dog!
An expression of enthusiasm or pleasure

in a nutshell
Describing a complicated situation in a few words

out of the frying pan and into the fire
Moving from a bad situation to one that is worse

piece of cake
Something that is easy to do

souped up
Made more fancy, improved in a cool way

spill the beans
Tell a secret

take it with a grain of salt
Expect that the information you've been given might not be true or complete

Eating
Through the Ages

Believe it or not, the ancient Egyptians and Greeks did not have fast food! That's right, they never experienced the joy of a burger served from a window to a person sitting in a car. Of course, they didn't have cars, either. Anyway, here's a look back at how much the foods people eat have changed (or not changed) through the millennia.

Ancient Egypt (about 3,500 years ago)

People ate bread made from emmer wheat; beer made from barley; fruits such as grapes, dates, figs, and melons; vegetables such as cucumbers, lettuce, onions, and garlic. Egyptians also discovered how to make marshmallows and that licorice was tasty.

Ancient Greece (about 2,500 years ago)

People ate *maza* bread made from barley and *artos* bread made from wheat. Olives were the most popular fruit, and olive oil came with most meals. Lentil soup was popular, as were figs and eggs. Fish was popular, along with squid and shellfish, but meat from animals was usually eaten only on special occasions.

Ancient Rome (2,000 years ago)

Wheat made into bread or porridge (called *puls*) was a big part of everyone's diet. Beans were common, too. Fish was available in most places, but meat was rarely served. Wine mixed with water was usually served with meals, along with yogurt. Rich folks enjoyed rare spices brought back by Rome's conquering armies. And yes, even back then, they ate pizza in Italy – it was a flatbread topped with vegetables or cheese. (No tomato sauce, though; that vegetable didn't come over from the Americas until about 1,500 years later.)

Europe (about 1,000 years ago)
This was a very poor time, and most folks could afford little more than barley bread and what veggies they could grow themselves. Since they ate so poorly, their teeth were bad, so any meat they got was usually turned into squishy hash.

Ancient Incas (1,000 years ago)
Potatoes and corn were the most common food; they added peppers, spices, and mint for flavor. The Incas also ate squash, tomatoes, avocados, and beans of various sorts. Grains included quinoa and amaranth. The Inca people chewed kaolin, a type of clay, when they got an upset stomach. They also preserved llama meat into what they called *charqui*, which is where we get the word *jerky*, meaning dried meat.

Mongol Dynasty (about 700 years ago)
Most of the foods these folks in Asia ate came from herd animals like cattle. They ate a lot of cheese and milk, along with the meat of the animals. A broth called *shülen* was made with meat, bones, and grains. The tasty dessert we call baklava came from this era; to make it, layers of paper-thin dough are piled up with honey, nuts, dates, and sugar.

Early America (400 years ago)
Archaeological digs at Jamestown found that early colonists ate tons of fish and turtles. They also ate herons, gulls, and raccoons. As other colonies became more settled, they grew grains such as barley and wheat. Colonies along different parts of the East Coast drew on their local land for meat, game, fish, and birds. Meat was a big part of most meals; not too many vegetables, so you might have liked living back then!

Food
Game Page

We've got ourselves a kitchen disaster! The chef accidentally threw tonight's entire meal into the blender. Look at the ugly jumble of letters below and see if you can find a complete dinner in there somewhere. Each letter is used only once, and you should be able to find a main course, a vegetable, a side dish, a drink, and a dessert. Put on your bib and dig in!

CHAPTER NINE

Grab Bag

What, you thought we could fit everything in the world into the other eight chapters? As if! Fortunately, we've got this chapter into which we can cram all the other cool stuff that didn't fit into the other eight.
Sort of like the junk drawer in your house. . . .

MOST
Dangerous Jobs

Police officers, firefighters, bodyguards: They certainly have dangerous jobs. They all put their lives on the line every day. But statistics show that it's the men and women listed here who have the most dangerous jobs in America.

1. Loggers
2. Aircraft pilots
3. Fishers and fishing workers
4. Structural iron and steel workers
5. Refuse and recyclable material collectors
6. Farmers and ranchers
7. Roofers
8. Electrical power line installers/repairers
9. Truck drivers
10. Taxi drivers and chauffeurs

Smelliest Jobs

Lots of people think their job stinks. But these literally do!

1. Manure inspector

Yes, there are scientists who collect animal manure to study bacteria. This was named one of the worst jobs in science by *Popular Science* magazine in 2005.

2. Wastewater diver

According to the *Washington Post*, four people have this job in Mexico City. They brave stinky, rancid waters to keep the city's pumps and sewers clear.

3. Crime scene cleanup

It's a dirty, depressing job, but people in the business say the lingering smell may be the worst part.

4. Roadkill cleanup

Somebody has to remove the carcasses from the middle of the highway.

5. Portable toilet cleaner

No explanation necessary.

There's a popular TV show called *Dirty Jobs* that has featured some other really stinky ways to make a living. The host heads into the field (often in protective gear) to find out what it's like to be a sludge cleaner, a worm dung farmer, a food recycler, a skull cleaner, or even an avian vomitologist, who studies owl vomit.

What Months Are Named For

January is the gateway to a new year — which is why the month is named for the Roman god of doors and gates. Here's how each month got its name.

MONTH	NAMED FOR
January	Janus, the Roman god of doors and gates.
February	The Roman word *februalia*, which means "purification." In this month, the Romans held their festival of purification.
March	Mars, the Roman god of war. Mars was also the protector of crops and fields, and March marks the beginning of spring.
April	The Latin word *aperire*, which means "to open" (this is the time of year that flower buds open).
May	Maia, the Roman goddess of bounty.
June	Juno, the Roman goddess of marriage.
July	The Roman emperor Julius Caesar.
August	The Roman emperor Augustus Caesar.
September	The Latin word *septem*, which means "seven." This was the seventh month of the ancient Roman year.
October	The Latin word *octem*, which means "eight." This was the eighth month of the ancient Roman year.
November	The Latin word *novem*, which means "nine." This was the ninth month of the ancient Roman year.
December	The Latin word *decem*, which means "ten." This was the tenth month of the ancient Roman year.

DAYS OF THE Week

Sunday's origin lies in the sun, and Monday's in the moon, but the rest of the days of the week aren't so obvious. Here's how each day got its name.

DAY	NAMED FOR
Sunday	Sunne, the German goddess of the sun.
Monday	Mani, the German god of the moon.
Tuesday	Tyr (in Old English, the name was Tiu or Tew), the Norse god of war.
Wednesday	Odin (in German mythology, the name was Woden), the chief god in Norse mythology.
Thursday	Thor, the Norse god of thunder.
Friday	Freya, the Norse goddess of love and beauty.
Saturday	Saturn, the Roman god of agriculture.

 Things are different in Turkmenistan. Its ruler, Saparmurat Niyazov, renamed January after his title, "Turkmenbashi," and April after his mom. Tuesday is "Young Day," Wednesday is now "Favorable Day," and Sunday is "Spirit Day."

MORE
Wild Phobias

Here's one more item we need to add to this ever-expanding list: a fear of phobias. Yes, there's a name for that, too! It's phobophobia.

Arachibutyrophobia
IS THE FEAR OF peanut butter sticking to the roof of your mouth

Blennophobia
IS THE FEAR OF slime

Defecaloesiophobia
IS THE FEAR OF painful bowel movements

Eisoptrophobia
IS THE FEAR OF seeing yourself in a mirror

Hippopotomonstrosesquippedaliophobia
IS THE FEAR OF long words

Liticaphobia
IS THE FEAR OF lawsuits

Novercaphobia
IS THE FEAR OF your stepmother

Octophobia
IS THE FEAR OF number 8

Paraskavedekatriaphobia
IS THE FEAR OF Friday the 13th

Pteronophobia
IS THE FEAR OF being tickled by feathers

Most Common
Last Names

It's no surprise that with more than 1.3 billion residents, China has the most common surnames (that's a fancy word for what most people use as last names) in the world: Li, Wang, Zhang, Liu, and Chen (and their variations). Here are the most common last names in the United States.

1. Smith
2. Johnson
3. Williams
4. Jones
5. Brown
6. Davis
7. Miller
8. Wilson
9. Moore
10. Taylor

11. Anderson
12. Thomas
13. Jackson
14. White
15. Harris
16. Martin
17. Thompson
18. Garcia
19. Martinez
20. Robinson

Boy Scout and Girl Scout Ranks

Planning to join the Boy Scouts or Girl Scouts? Then be prepared to rise through these ranks, starting with the lowest.

BOY SCOUT RANKS:

1. Scout Badge
2. Tenderfoot
3. Second Class
4. First Class
5. Star
6. Life
7. Eagle

Note: Eagle Palms are earned after becoming an Eagle Scout.

GIRL SCOUT RANKS:

1. Daisy
2. Brownie
3. Junior
4. Girl Scout
5. Adult

FAVORITE
Playground Games

All you need are two or more kids, some free time, and open space to play one of the oldest and most fun playground games ever: tag. Here are some other popular favorites that have stood the test of time.

1. Capture the Flag

2. Chinese Jump Rope

3. Four Square

4. Ghost in the Graveyard

5. Handball

6. Hide and Seek

7. Hopscotch

8. Pickle (Monkey in the Middle)

9. Red Light, Green Light

10. Wiffle Ball

Most Expensive Items
Sold on eBay

A round of golf with Tiger Woods was sold for $425,000 on the online auction site eBay. That almost seems like a bargain compared to these items.

	ITEM	PRICE
1.	340-year-old copy of Shakespeare's *Pericles, Prince of Tyre*	**$9,300,000**
2.	Grumman Gulfstream II jet	**$4,900,000**
3.	San Lorenzo 80 motor yacht	**$1,935,300**
4.	1909 Honus Wagner baseball card	**$1,265,000**
5.	Kentucky's Diamond Lake Resort	**$1,200,000**

One Amazing Place

Since it was launched in 1999, eBay has become a major part of world commerce. More used cars are sold through eBay than any other place. People use the site to sell just about anything you can think of. In 2004, someone sold a complete 50,000-year-old mammoth skeleton (named Max). More than 125 million people use the site regularly and many people have started small businesses doing nothing but buying and selling. It works pretty simply: Once you're registered (and you need a credit card!), you offer items and anyone can bid on them. At the end of the auction, the highest price gets the item; you get paid and then ship it.

What's in
Toothpaste?

We'll spare you the technical names of the ingredients, which can vary from brand to brand, but here's what is in that paste you brush your teeth with (after every meal, of course!).

Abrasives
Removes plaque and stains, and polishes teeth

Coloring agents
Turns plain toothpaste into a rainbow of colors

Detergents
Creates foaming action (or else the paste would dribble out of your mouth!)

Flavoring agents/sweeteners
Covers up the natural taste of the toothpaste (especially the yucky detergents)

Fluoride
Helps protect against cavities and strengthens tooth enamel

Humectants
Keeps toothpaste from drying out

Preservatives
Keeps toothpaste fresh and means you don't have to keep it in the fridge

Thickeners
Gives the paste texture

Barbie®'s Careers

From sports to politics to public service, there's almost nothing the famous (and talented!) doll hasn't tried. Here are just some of her many areas of expertise.

1. **Actress**
(and singer and rock star, too)
2. **Army officer**
(Air Force, Marine Corps, and Navy)
3. **Astronaut**
4. **Babysitter**
5. **Ballerina**
6. **Basketball player**
7. **Circus star**
8. **Dentist**
9. **Doctor**
10. **Fashion model**
(and designer and photographer, too)
11. **Firefighter**
12. **Flight attendant**
13. **Lifeguard**
14. **Nurse**
15. **Olympic gymnast**
(and figure skater)
16. **Paleontologist**
17. **Police officer**
18. **Presidential candidate**
19. **Teacher**
20. **Veterinarian**

THINGS
People Race

People have raced cars and bicycles and boats pretty much since the first time they hit the road (or the sea, depending). But folks will race just about anything, including these unusual vehicles.

1. Bathtubs
2. 18-wheel trucks
3. Golf carts
4. Kinetic sculptures
5. Lawn mowers
6. Shopping carts
7. Soapboxes
8. Toilets
9. Tractors
10. Wheelbarrows

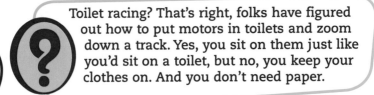

Toilet racing? That's right, folks have figured out how to put motors in toilets and zoom down a track. Yes, you sit on them just like you'd sit on a toilet, but no, you keep your clothes on. And you don't need paper.

Land Speed Records

Andy Green, a fighter pilot for Britain's Royal Air Force, broke the sound barrier when he set the current land speed record (the record for going the fastest on dry land) in 1997. He did it in a rocket-powered car. Here are the record holders at various selected intervals.

DATE	CAR/DRIVER	MPH/KPH
Dec. 18, 1898	Jeantaud/Gaston Chasseloup-Laubat	39.24/63.15
Jan. 17, 1899	Jenatzy/Camille Jenatzy	41.42/66.66
Mar. 4, 1899	Jeantaud/Gaston Chasseloup-Laubat	57.60/92.70
Apr. 29, 1899	Jenatzy/Camille Jenatzy	65.79/105.88
Apr. 13, 1902	Serpollet/Leon Serpollet	75.06/120.80
Jul. 17, 1903	Gobron-Brillie/Arthur Duray	83.47/134.33
Mar. 31, 1904	Gobron-Brillie/Louis Rigolly	94.78/152.53
Jul. 21, 1904	Gobron-Brillie/Louis Rigolly	103.55/166.65
Jul. 21, 1925	Sunbeam/Malcolm Campbell	150.76/242.62
Mar. 29, 1927	Sunbeam/Henry Segrave	203.79/327.97
Feb. 24, 1932	Bluebird/Malcolm Campbell	253.97/408.72
Sept. 3, 1935	Bluebird/Malcolm Campbell	301.13/484.62
Sept. 15, 1938	Railton/John Cobb	350.20/563.59
Jul. 17, 1964	Bluebird/Donald Campbell	403.10/648.73
Oct. 5, 1964	Wingfoot Express/Tom Green	434.02/698.49
Oct. 13, 1964	Spirit of America/Craig Breedlove	468.72/754.33
Oct. 15, 1964	Spirit of America/Craig Breedlove	526.28/846.97
Oct. 27, 1964	Green Monster/Art Arfons	536.71/863.75
Nov. 2, 1965	Spirit of America-Sonic I/Craig Breedlove	555.48/893.96
Nov. 7, 1965	Green Monster/Art Arfons	576.55/927.87
Nov. 15, 1965	Spirit of America-Sonic I/Craig Breedlove	600.60/966.57
Oct. 23, 1970	Blue Flame/Gary Gabelich	622.41/1,001.67
Oct. 4, 1983	Thrust 2/Richard Noble	633.47/1,019.47
Oct. 15, 1997	Thrust SSC/Andy Green	763.04/1,227.99

U.F.O. Sightings

Is there life out there in space? Here are 10 of the most well-known sightings of U.F.O.s (Unidentified Flying Objects). Have you ever seen one? Or are you a space alien yourself? If so, please contact us — we've got a lot of questions to ask you!

June 1947: While piloting his plane, Kenneth Arnold spotted a formation of unidentified aircraft and unwittingly coined the term "flying saucer."

July 1947: Not long after the Kenneth Arnold incident, the remnants of what was originally reported as a crashed "flying disk" were recovered near Roswell, New Mexico.

EARTH NEXT RIGHT

September 1961: While vacationing in Canada, New Hampshire's Betty and Barney Hill claimed to be "spacenapped" by a U.F.O.

April 1964: Lonnie Zamora, a police officer in Socorro, New Mexico, saw a strange craft and two individuals the size of small adults or children in white coveralls.

January 1969: Future president Jimmy Carter, then the governor of Georgia, spotted a U.F.O. outside the Lions Club in Leary, Georgia, where he was to give a speech.

September 1976: An Iranian Air Force pilot gave chase to an unidentified aircraft over Tehran. He could not fire a missile because his instrumentation was disabled. A second pilot had the same mechanical trouble until the U.F.O. left them behind.

December 1980: Betty Cash and two others driving through Piney Woods, Texas, saw a diamond-shaped object in the sky, soon followed by nearly two dozen military helicopters.

January 1981: French farmer Renato Nicolai spotted a small flying disk while working in his yard. It touched down, leaving behind changes in the landscape that authorities could not explain.

November 1989: A large, triangular craft quietly moved across the landscape of Belgium. Over the next several months, more than 1,000 sightings were reported.

March 1997: Numerous witnesses reported a series of unexplained lights moving in formation across the Arizona sky.

Famous Ghosts &

If you feel like ghost-hunting, here are a few places to start — and a few spirits to look for. Numerous people have claimed to have seen or heard ghosts or spirits in these places . . . but we're still waiting for the first photos or videos.

Famous Ghosts

1. **Caligula**   The emperor who is said to haunt the Lamian Gardens of Rome

2. **Anne Boleyn**   The second wife of King Henry VIII reportedly haunts stately Blickling Hall in Britain

3. **Abraham Lincoln**   The former president supposedly still roams the White House

4. **Marilyn Monroe**   The actress is one of several ghosts reportedly seen at Hollywood's famous Roosevelt Hotel

5. **Sir Walter Raleigh**   The famous writer, poet, and explorer is said to haunt the Tower of London, where he was imprisoned before being beheaded by King James

Haunted Places

Haunted Places

1. **The White House**   Washington, D.C.

2. **Tower of London**   Britain

3. **Alcatraz**   San Francisco, California

4. **The *Queen Mary***   The ocean liner docked in Long Beach, California

5. **The French Quarter**   New Orleans, Louisiana

Ghostly Presidents

Ghosts in the White House? Is the president safe? Well, probably so. Since it was built in the early 1800s, the White House has supposedly been home to several ghosts. Visitors, First Families, and guests have all reported seeing such strange sights as Abigail Adams doing her laundry; Dolly Madison hovering over the Rose Garden; and Abraham Lincoln wandering the hallways. The ghostly voice of David Burns, who owned the land on which the White House is built, has also been heard. Spooky!

Fastest Cars
You Can Buy

Forbes magazine found these cars to be the fastest that you can buy. Just be prepared to spend a few hundred thousand dollars for each one!

CAR	TOP SPEED (MPH/KPH)
1. Saleen S7 Twin Turbo	260/418
2. Koenigsegg CCR	242/389
3. Koenigsegg CC8S	240/386
4. Ultima Can-Am 640 & GTR 640	231/372
5. Spyker C8 Double 12 S	215/346
6. Mercedes-Benz SLR McLaren	207/333
7. Evans 387 & 487	206/331
8. Ford GT	205/330
9. Lamborghini Murciélago	205/330
10. Porsche Carrera GT	205/330

Useful Mnemonics

A mnemonic (pronounced *nee-MON-ik*) device is a helpful way to remember things. Here are a few worth, well . . . remembering.

Spring forward, fall back.
It comes in handy twice a year for remembering which way to adjust your clocks when the time changes.

***I* before e, except after *c*.**
To help with your spelling. The weird thing, though, is that there are a lot of exceptions to this rule.

Red sky at night, sailor's delight; red sky at morning, sailor's warning.
To help forecast the weather.

There's a rat in *separate*.
To remember how to spell this commonly misspelled word.

Richard of York gave battle in vain.
Use the first letter of each word to remember the colors of the rainbow: red, orange, yellow, green, blue, indigo, violet. You can also just remember the name Roy G. Biv.

Father Charles goes down and ends battle.
In music, take the first letter of each word to remember the order of the sharps: F, C, G, D, A, E, B.

Every good boy does fine.
Also in music, the ascending order of the notes in the treble clef: E, G, B, D, F.

My very eager mother served just us nuts.
The first letters are the initials, in order, of the planets. Until 2006, it ended "nine pizzas" to include Pluto.

Going Camping

It's not just about pitching a tent and roasting marshmallows anymore. These days, kids can find a summer camp for just about anything you can imagine. Here are just a few examples.

Acting camp

Cheerleading camp

Computer camp

Culinary camp

Filmmaking camp

Fitness camp

Rock 'n' roll camp

Scuba camp

Space camp

Theater camp

First Camps

The Boy Scouts of America was formed in 1910 as a way to give boys a fun activity. Their first summer camp was Camp Owasippe in Michigan. The Girl Scouts, formed in 1912 with similar ideas about helping kids have fun and learn, opened their first camp at Camp Bonnie Brae, in Massachusetts. Both camps are still welcoming Scouts from all over every summer.

Biggest Statues

New York's Statue of Liberty may be the most famous statue in the world, but it's not the tallest. That distinction belongs to a Buddha statue in Japan that is two-and-a-half times taller than the Statue of Liberty. Here are some other huge statues throughout the world.

STATUE/SITE	HEIGHT (FEET/METERS)
Amida Buddha/Ushiku, Japan	396/120
Mother Russia Statue/Volgograd, Russia	270/82.3
Lishan Buddha/Sichuan Province, China	220/67
Statue of Liberty/New York, New York	151/46
Wat Pho Buddha*/Bangkok, Thailand	151/46
Cosmoplanetary Messiah/Castellane, France	107/32.6
Christ Redeemer/Rio de Janeiro, Brazil	98/29.9

*This one is actually lying down, not standing up!

Here's a list of some cool facts about the Statue of Liberty:
- The total weight of copper and steel in the statue is 312,000 pounds (141,500 kg).
- There are 25 windows in the crown.
- One index finger alone is 8 feet (2.4 m).
- Liberty Island, where the statue is located, was once known as Bedloe's Island.

Knock, Knock

Here are our picks for the good and the bad in the world of knock-knock jokes. Of course, your opinion may vary!

Best

"Knock, knock."

"Who's there?"

"Interrupting cow."

"Interrupting cow—"

"Moooooooooo!"

"Knock, knock."

"Who's there?"

"Boo."

"Boo who?"

"Don't cry. It's only a knock-knock joke."

"Knock, knock."

"Who's there?"

"Nobel."

"Nobel who?"

"No bell, so I knocked!"

"Knock, knock."

"Who's there?"

"Little old lady."

"Little old lady who?"

"I didn't know you could yodel!"

"Knock, knock."

"Who's there?"

"Boyd."

"Boyd who?"

"Boy, do you ask a lot of questions!"

"Knock, knock."

"Who's there?"

"Police."

"Police who?"

"Police let us in. It's cold!"

Worst

Some knock-knock jokes are so bad that they're good. We'll let you decide if these qualify.

"Knock, knock."

"Who's there?"

"Lettuce."

"Lettuce who?"

"[sing] Let us entertain you. Let us make you smile!"

"Knock, knock."

"Who's there?"

"Who."

"Who who?"

"Uh-oh, there's an owl at the door!"

"Knock, knock."

"Who's there?"

"Toodle."

"Toodle who?"

"Good-bye!"

"Knock, knock."

"Who's there?"

"Banana."

"Banana who?"

"Knock, knock."

"Who's there?"

"Banana."

"Banana who?"

"Knock, knock."

"Who's there?"

"Orange."

"Orange who?"

"Orange you glad I didn't say banana?"

"Knock, knock."

"Who's there?"

"Atch."

"Atch who?"

"Gesundheit!"

That's Just Gross

Rings through the tongue? Intentional scarring? These real-life body modifications will make you say, "Ewwwww!" (or "Ouch!").

* In Myanmar (formerly known as Burma), women in the Padaung tribe stretch their necks by wearing a series of neck rings. They consider it a sign of beauty and stature.

* In some cultures (in certain tribes in Ethiopia and Brazil, for instance), large plates, or plugs, are inserted into the lower lip to stretch it far beyond the usual proportions.

✳ According to *Ripley's Believe It or Not!: Planet Eccentric,* the world's most-pierced woman lives in Brazil. Elaine Davidson has close to 2,000 piercings. She can put her finger through her tongue!

✳ Cuba's Luis Antonio Aguero is reportedly the world's most-pierced man. He has 230 body piercings.

✳ Remember Mr. Spock on television's *Star Trek*? A man in China had plastic surgery to give him the same pointy ears as the universe's most famous Vulcan.

✳ Dennis Avner of Whidbey Island, Washington, is better known as Catman or Stalking Cat. He's made many body alterations — including implants to allow for whiskers — so he can resemble a tiger.

✳ The Lizard Man is Erik Sprague, a performer whose many body modifications give him the appearance of a reptile. He's even got a bifurcated tongue — that means it's forked, like a lizard's.

Grab Bag
Game Page

It's a grab bag chapter . . . so we've got a grab bag game. There are six different puzzles below, all in different formats. Complete all the puzzles and then take the letters that end up in (or are already in) the shaded circles and unscramble them to find something from this chapter you put in your mouth. Note: All the answers to the various puzzles can be found in this chapter . . . somewhere!

1. Fill in the blank letters to find the mystery word:

__ __ M __ ◯O __ __ G __ S __

2. Unscramble these letters to find something from the chapter.

H H D T O D P W A A B U ____ ____ _____

3. Which item doesn't belong on the list?

Spyker, Evans, Porsche, Can-Am, Conor, Ford:

_____

4. Fill in the blanks of this mini word snake. Except for the first word, the first letter of each word is the last letter of the word ahead of it.

A. Gave his name to January   C. Job of July's name origin

B. Namesake of nearest star   D. Calendar we got four months from

Mystery word:

__ __ __ __ __ __ __ __ __

CHAPTER TEN

Sports

Banana slugs, a catch-can man, niblicks, spoons, sepak takraw, Saran Wrap, Salchows, and anteaters: What do all these have to do with sports? Read on to find out.

Greatest Athletes

A few years ago, as the 1900s turned into the 2000s, people created tons of "best-of-the-century" lists. This one is taken from a list of the best North American athletes of the 1900s, as chosen by a panel of experts brought together by ESPN. How many have you heard of? If you haven't, check 'em out . . . they were amazing.

Hank Aaron, baseball

Muhammad Ali, boxing

Jim Brown, football

Wilt Chamberlain, basketball

Ty Cobb, baseball

Babe Didrikson Zaharias, track & field and golf

Wayne Gretzky, ice hockey

Michael Jordan, basketball

Carl Lewis, track & field

Joe Louis, boxing

of the 20th Century

Willie Mays, baseball
Martina Navratilova, tennis
Jack Nicklaus, golf
Jesse Owens, track & field
Babe Ruth, baseball
Jim Thorpe,
track & field, baseball, and football
Jackie Robinson, baseball
Ted Williams, baseball

A Miracle Moment

Sports Illustrated magazine made a list, too, and named its top sports moments of the century. Number one was the victory of the U.S. hockey team over the heavily favored Soviet Union in the 1980 Winter Olympics.

Red Dogs AND Blitzes

Every sport has its own language, but football seems to create more unique terminology than most sports. *Touchdown* and *kickoff* you know, but here's a list of some unusual slang terms that will let you fit into any huddle you join.

Blitz On this defensive play, linebackers, cornerbacks, or safeties all rush the quarterback at the snap, instead of going back in pass coverage.

Hail Mary A long pass thrown up for grabs (like a prayer), often at the end of a half or a game.

Mike, Sam, and Will These are nicknames for the middle, strongside (opposite the tight end), and weakside linebackers.

Pancake A block by an offensive player that puts a defender flat on his back.

Read Just like you're reading this book, quarterbacks and coaches have to "read" a defense, trying to see how they're going to line up for a play.

Red dog A sort of old-fashioned name for a blitz.

The Rock The football.

Snot-bubbler A hit by a defender that is so hard the player with the ball has, um, something coming out of his nose.

Take it to the house Carry the ball into the end zone for a touchdown.

Thumper A defensive player adept at producing snot-bubblers.

NFL Uniform Rules

There's an old saying in sports: "You can't tell the players without a scorecard." Well, in the NFL that's only partly true. In 1973, the league put in place a numbering system, assigning numbers to each position group. The lastest change to the system came in 2004, when the league added receivers to the 10–19 group.

NUMBERS   POSITIONS

1–9 Quarterbacks and kickers

10–19 Quarterbacks, receivers, and kickers

20–49 Running backs and defensive backs

50–59 Centers and linebackers

60–79 Defensive linemen and offensive linemen

80–89 Receivers and tight ends

90–99 Defensive linemen and linebackers

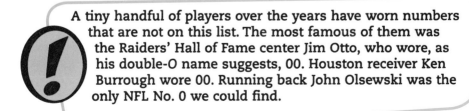

A tiny handful of players over the years have worn numbers that are not on this list. The most famous of them was the Raiders' Hall of Fame center Jim Otto, who wore, as his double-O name suggests, 00. Houston receiver Ken Burrough wore 00. Running back John Olsewski was the only NFL No. 0 we could find.

NBA Big & Small

Being tall is usually important for NBA players, so here's a list of the tallest of the tall, the most sky-high players in NBA history. But short players can succeed, too, with quickness and great ball-handling skills. So we've also got a list of the shortest players in league history. It just goes to show, it's not the size of the athlete, it's the size of his heart that counts — but being tall does help!

TALLEST

HEIGHT (FEET-INCHES/CM)	PLAYER
7-7/200	Manute Bol
	Gheorghe Muresan
7-6/198	Shawn Bradley
7-5/195	Chuck Nevitt
	Slavko Vranes
	Yao Ming
7-4/193	Mark Eaton
	Priest Lauderdale
	Ralph Sampson
	Rik Smits

SHORTEST

5-3/160	Muggsy Bogues
5-5/165	Earl Boykins
5-7/170	Jerry Dover
	Greg Grant
	Keith Jennings
	Herm Klotz
	Vat Misaka
	Monte Towe
	Spud Webb

Famous Dunks

The slam dunk is basketball's most popular play. Players seem to defy gravity as they soar through the air. Toss in some midair gymnastics and the power of the final slam into the basket, and you've got one crowd-pleasing maneuver. Here is a list of some of the most famous or important dunks in basketball history.

Jason Richardson, 2003

Voted by fans as the best-ever in the NBA's annual dunk contest, Richardson leaped, passed the ball between his legs, and then reached back behind his head to slam the ball home.

Lisa Leslie, 2002

The Los Angeles Sparks star made the first slam dunk in the history of the WNBA.

Vince Carter, 2000

At the Olympics, Carter leapfrogged over a 7-2 (218 cm) French player to dunk the ball.

Michael Jordan, 1991

So good he's on here twice: Jordan's dunk over Patrick Ewing in the playoffs was the number-one dunk on the 1999 DVD "NBA's 100 Greatest Plays."

Michael Jordan, 1988

During the NBA slam-dunk contest, "Air" Jordan leaped all the way from the free-throw line to the basket to slam it home!

Spud Webb, 1986

Though only 5-7, Spud had major hops. He won the slam-dunk contest with a 360-degree-spin slam.

Lorenzo Charles, 1983

This wasn't the prettiest, but perhaps the most important. Charles caught a missed shot and slammed it home as time expired to give North Carolina State an upset NCAA championship over Houston.

Julius "Dr. J" Erving, 1983

This early dunkmaster's 1983 slam over Kareem Abdul-Jabbar of the Lakers is an all-time great.

Baseball
by the Numbers

Baseball is a game simply chock-full of numbers. There are statistics for just about anything. If you want to know a player's average while batting left-handed on Tuesdays in May against right-handers in a domed stadium, you can find that out. But most of those numbers disappear quickly. Others stand the test of time and are as recognizable to longtime fans as the names of the players themselves. Here are a handful of baseball's most famous statistics.

NUMBER	MEANING
3	Uniform number of the great Babe Ruth
24	Uniform number of all-around star Willie Mays
56	Record number of consecutive games with a hit by Joe DiMaggio in 1941
61	Single-season home run total by Roger Maris in 1961, the record until Mark McGwire broke it in 1998
73	Current single-season homer mark, set by Barry Bonds in 2003
191	Single-season RBI record set by Hack Wilson in 1930
.366	All-time best career batting average of Ty Cobb
.406	1941 batting average of Ted Williams, the last man to hit above .400
511	Career-record pitching wins by Cy Young
755	All-time record home run total of Hank Aaron
2,130	Consecutive games played streak by Lou Gehrig, 1923–1939*
4,191**	Ty Cobb's career hits total, the record until Pete Rose broke it in 1985

*Gehrig held the record until 1995, when Cal Ripken, Jr. broke it. But Ripken's final total of 2,632 hasn't really gained the same fame . . . yet.

**Research in the 1990s found that this number, famous for decades, was wrong; Cobb's career total is now listed as 4,189. However, the 4,191 number is still much more well-known.

Perfect Games

In baseball, a perfect game is one in which a pitcher wins the game while retiring every single batter he faces. That is, not one opposing batter reaches base in any way: hit, error, walk, or whatever. In pro baseball's nearly 150-year history, there have been only 17 perfect games pitched (through 2005). Don Larsen's is the only one to have been pitched in the World Series.

PITCHER, TEAM	YEAR
J. Lee Richmond, Brown Stockings	1880
J. Montgomery Ward, Grays	1880
Cy Young, Red Sox	1904
Addie Joss, Indians	1908
Charley Robertson, Tigers	1922
Don Larsen, Yankees	1956
Jim Bunning, Phillies	1964
Jim "Catfish" Hunter, Athletics	1968
Len Barker, Indians	1981
Mike Witt, Angels	1984
Tom Browning, Reds	1988
Dennis Martinez, Expos	1991
Kenny Rogers, Rangers	1994
David Wells, Yankees	1998
David Cone, Yankees	1999
Randy Johnson, Diamondbacks	2004

Series Little & BIG

The goal of most Little League players is to reach the famous Little League World Series (LLWS) held each August in Williamsport, Pennsylvania. The goal of every baseball player is to make it to the major league World Series (WS), played every October between the American League and National League champs. This list includes the small set of players who have reached BOTH of those goals!

PLAYER	LLWS	FIRST WS (TEAM)
Boog Powell	1954	1966 (Orioles)
Jim Barbieri	1954	1966 (Orioles)
Rick Wise	1958	1975 (Red Sox)
Carney Lansford	1969	1990 (Athletics)
Ed Vosberg	1973	1997 (Marlins)
Charlie Hayes	1977	1996 (Yankees)
Dwight Gooden	1979	1986 (Mets)
Derek Bell	1980-81	1992 (Blue Jays)
Gary Sheffield	1980	1997 (Marlins)
Jason Marquis	1991	2004 (Cardinals)
Jason Varitek	1984	2004 (Red Sox)

Super Sluggers

Homer, tater, dinger, long ball, goin' yard, big fly, "Good-bye, Mr. Spalding" — whatever you call it (and there are dozens more nicknames), the home run is baseball's greatest hit. The players on this list of the all-time career home run leaders are among baseball's most famous and celebrated players. Going, going . . . gone!

PLAYER, TEAM	HOMERS*
Hank Aaron, Braves/Brewers	755
Barry Bonds**, Pirates/Giants	734
Babe Ruth, Yankees/Braves	714
Willie Mays, Giants/Mets	660
Sammy Sosa, White Sox/Cubs/Orioles	588
Frank Robinson, Orioles/Reds	586
Mark McGwire, A's/Cardinals	583
Harmon Killebrew, Senators/Twins	573
Rafael Palmeiro, Cubs/Rangers/Orioles	569
Reggie Jackson, A's/Angels/Yankees	563
Ken Griffey, Jr.**, Mariners/Reds	563
Mike Schmidt, Phillies	548
Mickey Mantle, Yankees	536
Jimmie Foxx, A's/Red Sox	534
Willie McCovey, Giants	521

*Statistics through 2006 season.   **Active through 2006.

Who's Who in the
Pit Crew

Did you ever notice that whenever they interview a NASCAR driver after the race, he always says "we"? He'll say, "We had a great race." Or "We drove well today." Who is he talking about? Was there someone else in the car with him? How many steering wheels does his car have, anyway? Well, of course, he's not talking about people in the car with him; he's all alone in there out on the track. He's talking about the important support team behind him: the pit crew. When he stops during a race, these highly trained experts leap into action. They can change four tires and fill up the gas tank in about 18 seconds! Each NASCAR pit crew has seven main members; here is a list of their jobs and responsibilities.

The Jack Man

He carries a long-handled floor jack. With one pump of the handle, he lifts one side of the car off the ground. After the tires are changed on that side, he lowers the car and sprints around to the other side. When the second pair of tires is changed, he checks his crew, drops the car, and signals the driver to take off.

Tire Carriers

One each for the front and rear – they lug new 80-pound (36-kg) tires over the wall separating the crew area from the track. After the old tires are removed, they quickly carry them back over the wall. The job demands balance and strength.

Tire Changers

Using an air gun, these two crew members – again, one each for the front and rear tires – remove the lug nuts that attach the tire to the car (they can unscrew five in about two seconds!), then hang a new tire and screw the nuts back on. Then they race around to the other side of the car and repeat the process.

Gas Can Man

At the rear of the car, this crew member empties two 11-gallon (41.6-l) containers of gasoline into the tank. He wears a special protective face mask because of fuel fumes, plus a fireproof apron.

Catch-Can Man

The gas can man's assistant hands him the full cans and takes away the empties. He helps catch any overflow fuel to prevent fires. He also stands ready to assist any other crew member who needs help.

Off the Track

A NASCAR team also includes:

• A crew chief, who supervises the entire team and communicates with the driver during the race

• Spotters, who sit high above the track and radio in reports from around the track

• Crew assistants, who use long poles to deliver water to the driver, clean the windshield, and clean debris off the front air grill

NASCAR's Tracks

NASCAR holds 36 races each season at tracks around the United States. The schedule changes slightly from year to year, but these tracks are almost always on the annual roster. Some of these tracks are the site of two or more races per season.

TRACK NAME	LOCATION
Atlanta Motor Speedway	Atlanta, Georgia
Bristol Motor Speedway	Bristol, Tennessee
California Speedway	Fontana, California
Chicagoland Speedway	Joliet, Illinois
Darlington Raceway	Darlington, South Carolina
Daytona International Speedway	Daytona Beach, Florida
Dover International Speedway	Dover, Delaware
Homestead-Miami Speedway	Homestead, Florida
Indianapolis Speedway	Indianapolis, Indiana
Infineon Raceway	Sonoma, California
Kansas Speedway	Kansas City, Kansas
Las Vegas Motor Speedway	Las Vegas, Nevada
Lowe's Motor Speedway	Charlotte, North Carolina
Martinsville Speedway	Martinsville, Virginia
Michigan International Speedway	Brooklyn, Michigan
New Hampshire International Speedway	Loudon, New Hampshire
Talladega Superspeedway	Talladega, Alabama
Texas Motor Speedway	Justin, Texas
Phoenix International Raceway	Phoenix, Arizona
Pocono Raceway	Long Pond, Pennsylvania
Richmond International Raceway	Richmond, Virginia
Watkins Glen International	Watkins Glen, New York

NASCAR's
Families

Since its beginnings in 1948, NASCAR has always included many families among its driving teams. Fathers and sons, brothers, cousins, even sisters have all taken part in NASCAR races. In fact, one family, the Frances, has owned NASCAR since its founding. This list includes just a few of the more prominent NASCAR families (listed from oldest to youngest members).

Bodine
Geoffrey, Brett, Todd

Earnhardt
Ralph, Dale Sr.*, Dale Jr., Kerry

Flock
Tim*, Fonty, Bob, Ethel

Jarrett
Ned*, Dale*

Labonte
Terry*, Bobby*

Petty
Lee*, Richard*, Kyle, Adam

Wallace
Rusty*, Mike, Kenny

Waltrip
Darrell*, Michael

*Won at least one NASCAR season championship

BIZARRE
College Nicknames

On the following page, you'll see just how boring many colleges and universities can be in deciding what their sports team mascot or nickname will be. But on this page, we celebrate creativity. We enjoy the fun and the silly. We honor the weird! Here are some actual nicknames or mascots of American colleges that make rooting for their sports teams that much more fun. Go Slugs!

NICKNAME	SCHOOL
Anteaters	Univ. of Calif. at Irvine
Artichokes	Scottsdale Comm. College
Billikens	St. Louis Univ.
Demon Deacons	Wake Forest Univ.
Dirt Bags*	Calif. State Univ. at Long Beach
Ephs	Williams College
Fightin' Banana Slugs	Univ. of Calif. at Santa Cruz
Fighting Blue Hens	Univ. of Delaware
Geoducks**	Evergreen State College
Golden Gophers	Univ. of Minnesota
Hatters	Stetson Univ.
Hokies	Virginia Tech
Hoyas	Georgetown Univ.
Humpback Whales	Univ. of Alaska-Southeast
Ladies/Gentlemen***	Centenary College
Mean Green	Univ. of North Texas
Ragin' Cajuns	Univ. of Louisiana-Lafayette
Ramblin' Wreck	Georgia Tech
Thundering Herd	Marshall Univ.
Wheatshockers	Wichita State
Zips	Akron Univ.

*Baseball team only **Pronounced "GOO-ee-ducks"

***Men's and women's teams, of course

Eagles and Tigers and Knights, Oh My!

Now that you've seen how colleges can have fun with their nicknames (page 292), here is a list of the most popular nicknames among colleges and universities in the United States (at least 20 schools have each nickname). The National Collegiate Athletic Association (NCAA) does not keep an official list, but we checked a variety of sources to come up with this "most popular" list. (Also, we didn't include the various "Fighting"s, "Golden"s, or "Runnin'"s that some schools add to their names.)

NICKNAME/NUMBER OF SCHOOLS

Eagles/52
Tigers/44
Bulldogs/38
Cougars/32
Wildcats/32
Pioneers/31
Lions/30
Panthers/30
Crusaders/27
Warriors/26
Knights/25
Bears/24
Saints/20

BAD
Sports Records

Holding a sports record is usually a great honor. Being the best at something or having the most of something is normally something to brag about. However, there are some records in sports that no one wants to hold. But guess what? Someone has to! On these pages, read about some of the least popular records in sports and meet the unfortunate record-holders. You can look it up (but most of these folks would probably prefer you didn't!).

FOOTBALL

Most fumbles in a game
7, Len Dawson, 1964

Throwing most interceptions in a game
8, Jim Hardy, 1950

Throwing most interceptions in a season
42, George Blanda, 1962

Most times sacked in a season
76, David Carr, 2001

Most consecutive losses (team)
26, Tampa Bay Buccaneers, 1976-1977

BASEBALL

Most errors in an inning
6, Joe Mulvey (3B), 1884

Most errors in a career
972, Bill Dahlen (SS)

Most home runs allowed in a career
505, Robin Roberts

Most grounding into double plays, career
350, Cal Ripken, Jr.

Most strikeouts (by a batter) in a season
195, Adam Dunn, 2004

Most losses in a season (team)
134, Cleveland Spiders, 1899

BASKETBALL

Worst free-throw percentage in a career (min. 1,200 free throws made)
Wilt Chamberlain, 51.1 percent

Most turnovers in a season
366, Artis Gilmore, 1977-1978

Most losses in a season (team)
73, Philadelphia 76ers, 1972-1973

ICE HOCKEY

Most goals allowed by one team in game:
16, Quebec Bulldogs, vs. Montreal, March 3, 1920

Most penalty minutes in a season
472, Dave "Tiger" Schultz, 1974-1975

Most career losses by a goalie
352, Gump Worsley

HORSE RACING

Most consecutive losses
100, Zippy Chippy, 1992-2004

MAJOR LEAGUE
Soccer Champs

Inspired by the success of the 1994 soccer World Cup, held in the United States for the first time, Major League Soccer (MLS) was launched in 1996. It was not the first pro soccer league in America, but it has become the most successful. For the 2006 season, it had 12 teams playing across the country. Here is a list of winners of the annual MLS Cup, the league's championship.

YEAR	MLS CHAMPION
2006	Houston Dynamo
2005	Los Angeles Galaxy
2004	D.C. United
2003	San Jose Earthquakes
2002	Los Angeles Galaxy
2001	San Jose Earthquakes
2000	Kansas City Wizards
1999	D.C. United
1998	Chicago Fire
1997	D.C. United
1996	D.C. United

? Why is the team in Washington called "D.C. United"? When MLS was being formed, some teams looked to the traditional European teams for inspiration for their names. Several long-playing clubs in Britain use "United" in their name, such as Manchester United. The name came from when athletic groups combined several local clubs to create a city's top club.

OVERSEAS Americans

While Major League Soccer has become a key source of talent for the U.S. National Team, many top American players still look to Europe to gain experience. In 2006, a record number of U.S. players earned their soccer paychecks playing for top European pro clubs. When these guys play, they pack their passports along with their soccer cleats.

PLAYER, POSITION	EUROPEAN TEAM, COUNTRY
DaMarcus Beasley, MF	PSV Eindhoven, Netherlands
Gregg Berhalter, D	1860 Munich, Germany
Carlos Bocanegro, D	FC Fulham, England
Danny Califf, M	Aalborg BK, Denmark
Conor Casey, F	FSV Mainz 05, Germany
Steve Cherundolo, D	Hannover 96, Germany
Bobby Convey, MF	Reading, England
Jay DeMerit, D	Watford, England
Brad Friedel, GK	Blackburn Rovers, England
Marcus Hahnemann, GK	Reading, England
Tim Howard, GK	Manchester United, England
Kasey Keller, GK	Borussia Mönchengladbach, Germany
Eddie Lewis, MF	Leeds United, England
Brian McBride, F	FC Fulham, England
Oguchi Onyewu, D	Standard de Liege, Belgium
Claudio Reyna, MF	Manchester City, England

Positions: D, defender; MF, midfielder; F, forward; GK, goalkeeper

MR. AND MS.
Everythings

For some athletes, it's not enough to be world-class at just one sport. These multitalented superstars excelled in two or more sports. They didn't just play in other sports, they were among the best in both. The hardest part of their lives was probably keeping all the uniforms straight!

Jeremy Bloom
Outstanding college wide receiver; Olympic moguls skier

Jim Brown
Hall of Fame member in both NFL and college lacrosse

Bo Jackson
All-star baseball player; Pro Bowl running back

Marion Jones
Olympic gold-medal sprinter; great college basketball player

Jackie Robinson
First four-sport star at UCLA; baseball Hall of Famer

Deion Sanders
Top football cornerback; baseball outfielder

Jim Thorpe
Olympic gold medal winner in heptathlon and decathlon; NFL Hall of Famer; pro baseball player

Babe Didrikson Zaharias
Olympic champion in track; golfing superstar

Spoons & Niblicks!

Golfers today can carry 14 clubs in their golf bags during an official round. The three main types of clubs are woods (though they're all made of metal now), irons, and putters. The woods and irons are numbered, in most cases. You use a 1-wood, or driver, to tee off, then perhaps hit a 5-iron toward the green. Once on the green, you use a putter. In the early days of golf, however, all the clubs had names. They don't match up exactly with the numbered clubs of today in how they were made or what they looked like, but these are the approximate comparisons between yesterday (before the 1920s or so) and today. So, where did I put my niblick?

OLD NAME	SIMILAR CLUB TODAY
Play club	Driver
Brassie	2-wood
Spoon	3-4-5-woods
Baffing spoon	6-7-8-woods
Cleek	1- or 2-iron
Mid mashie	3-iron
Mashie iron	4-iron
Mashie	5-iron
Spade	6-iron
Mashie niblick	7-iron
Pitching niblick	8-iron
Niblick	9-iron
Jigger	Wedge
Putter (or blank)	Putter

Famous
Sports Streaks

The "streak" has always fascinated sports fans. An athlete's ability to succeed over and over again, against all the odds and opponents, places them above the rest. Some streaks are team achievements, when skill, determination, and yes, luck all come together to help a team win again and again. Here are some of the most famous streaks in sports history.

Baseball

Joe DiMaggio hit safely in 56 consecutive games, 1941.

Lou Gehrig played in 2,130 consecutive games, 1923–1939.

Cal Ripken, Jr., broke Gehrig's record with a total of 2,632, 1982–1998.

The Boston Red Sox won eight straight postseason games to win the World Series, 2004.

Basketball

The Los Angeles Lakers won 33 games in a row, 1971–1972.

UCLA's basketball team won 88 games in a row, 1971–1974, and nine of 10 NCAA basketball titles, 1964–1973.

Cycling

Lance Armstrong won seven straight Tour de France races, 1999–2005.

Football
The Miami Dolphins won 17 games in a row, the NFL's only undefeated season, 1972.

The University of Oklahoma won 47 straight games, 1953–1957.

Hockey
Wayne Gretzky was the NHL's most valuable player eight straight years, 1980–1987.

Golf
Tiger Woods made the cut (qualified for the final rounds) in 142 consecutive tournaments, 1998–2005.

Tennis
Martina Navratilova set a women's record with 74 consecutive match victories, 1984.

Track and Field
Al Oerter won the discus event at four consecutive Olympics, 1956–1968.

Edwin Moses won 107 straight 400-meter hurdle races, 1977–1987.

So, which of these streaks is the most unbreakable? Fans of American sports would probably look to DiMaggio's record; since 1941, no player has come closer than 12 games to his mark. In team sports, UCLA's record is probably toughest, since few of the best players stay in college long enough to help break it. Around the world, Armstrong's mark is probably unbeatable. But you never know!

Tour de France
Champions

The Tour de France bicycle race is perhaps the most grueling and difficult challenge in sports. Over the course of about a month, riders cover about 2,000 miles (3,200 km) in a series of daily rides, often climbing thousands of feet up steep mountain roads. The race demands great skill, enormous stamina, and supreme dedication. When American Lance Armstrong finally hung up his cycling helmet after winning his record seventh Tour in 2005, he found himself atop this list of multiple Tour de France winners.

Cyclist, Country	Tour de France Wins
Lance Armstrong, USA	7
Bernard Hinault, France	5
Eddy Merckx, Belgium	5
Miguel Indurain, Spain	5
Jacques Anquetil, France	5
Greg LeMond, USA	3
Louis Bobet, France	3
Phillipe Thys, Belgium	3

Figure Skating
MOVES

Every sport has its own language, of course, but figure skating seems to have some of the most colorful. Here is a list of some of the most well-known names of maneuvers used by figure skaters during their routines.

TYPES OF JUMPS

Axel
Flip
Lutz
Salchow
Toe loop
Walley
Waltz jump

TYPES OF SPINS

Biellman
Broken leg spin
Camel
Death drop spin
Flying camel
Flying sit spin
Layback
Sit spin

Your Name in Ice

Several of these moves take their name from their inventors. Ulrich Salchow won the world championship 10 times early in the 20th century. Axel Paulson was the 1908 Olympic champion. Alois Lutz invented the backward jump that bears his name. American Dorothy Hamill perfected a version of an older trick; hers was dubbed a "Hamill Camel."

Odd Balls

Most sports use round (or should we say "spherical?") balls — golf balls, tennis balls, basketballs, bowling balls, volleyballs, etc. Footballs are a little different, of course. (Here's some great trivia for you, by the way. Do you know what the shape of a football is called? Amaze your friends by knowing that it's a "prolate spheroid.") But not every sport bounces to the tune of a round ball. Here's a list of some pieces of unusual sports equipment that are used sort of like a ball — they are thrown, kicked, batted, hit, or otherwise tossed — but look very little like the balls you're used to.

Birdie

Not thrown but hit with a badminton racket, birdies (or "shuttlecocks") are made of feathers or plastic and are shaped like cones.

Curling stone

Slid along the ice in the sport of curling, the round stone has a flat bottom and a handle on top.

Discus

Shaped like a bulging dinner plate, the discus is thrown after a spinning run-up.

Earthball

About 6 ft. (1.8 m) in diameter and made of canvas, it is used in playground games.

Hammer

A shot put (see opposite page) at the end of a 3-ft. (1-m) chain or wire, it is thrown after a spinning run-up.

Javelin

A thin, metal, spear-like pole thrown for distance.

Medicine ball

This is a heavy leather or plastic ball filled with sand or liquid that is used for exercising.

Road bowling ball

A solid iron ball about twice the size of a golf ball, this ball is used in an Irish sport that is contested on roads between towns.

Sepak takraw

Made of woven wicker, wood, or plastic, it is used in an Asian foot-tennis game.

Shot put

An iron ball weighing 8–16 lbs. (4–7.2 kg), it is thrown for distance in a track-and-field event.

Mega Moto X

Daring, brave, or just crazy — Moto X riders have taken the aerial stunts of BMX bicycles and turned them into high-flying, supercharged vertical ballets. Gunning their motorcycles off ramps, they fly through the air, doing any one of dozens of types of gymnastic tricks in midair. They land safely (we hope) and their moves are scored by judges. Here is how the hotshots do a few of the hot Moto X tricks you might see at events such as the X Games or Winter X Games.

Backflip
Do a 360-degree (complete circle) backward loop.

Bar Hop
Put both feet on the handlebars and then get them back down before landing.

Coffin
Lie on your back and hold your feet out forward, while still holding on to the handlebars.

Nothing
Take your hands and feet off the bike and then get them back on (quickly!) before landing.

Saran Wrap
Circle one foot under each hand, one after the other.

Superman
Keep your hands on the handlebars but straighten your body out parallel to the ground.

Twitch
Stick one leg out to the side and one leg over the handlebars while in flight.

Whip
Keep your hands and feet on the bike, but turn the bike so that it's "lying down" in midair; straighten up before landing.

Ironpeople

A triathlon is a race in which competitors swim, bike, and run over varying distances. The ultimate triathlon length is the mighty Ironman, the most famous of which is in Hawaii. In an Ironman triathlon, men and women first swim 2.4 miles (3.8 km) in an open, rough, and choppy ocean. Climbing out, they hop on racing bikes and pedal for 112 miles (180 km). As if that was not enough, they then wrap up their day with a marathon — 26 miles, 385 yards (42 km) of grueling running. The best can finish in about eight hours. Now that's a tough day at the office. Here's a list of some of the most successful Hawaii Ironman competitors since the first race was held in 1978.

IRONPERSON	NO. OF RACES WON
Paula Newby-Fraser	8
Dave Scott	6
Mark Allen	6
Natascha Badmann	6
Peter Reid	3
Scott Tinley	2
Tim DeBoom	2
Luc Van Lierde	2
Lori Bowden	2
Erin Baker	2

SPORTS

Sports
Game Page

For our last game, we'll test your knowledge of the sports stuff you've read in this chapter. There are three "odd balls," five NASCAR families, five female athletes (last names only), five baseball teams, and five MLS teams. (For the teams, use nicknames; such as *Bears*, not *Chicago Bears*.) If you can't track them down without a list, check out the answer list on page 319 (but no peeking at the answer grid!).

```
R S N A I D N I Q S E T
E D A V S I D E T I N U
J A V E L I N I E O L W
O L R S T P G W A T L A
N L A R Q E T N O B A L
E I T D R T E F N I B L
S M I S A T D Z V F H A
G A L A X Y A W W L T C
S H O R A H A Z I O R E
H A V M A L X O Z C A Y
R E A R T H Q U A K E S
E F I R D E I N R D X T
D A I L R J G I D M Y H
S P M I S E D I S C U S
O O F D L E D V T A S U
X O S S E J L S H E N E
```

308

Index

Games Answer Page

HISTORY, page 44

1. 1918	6. 1777
2. 1984	7. 161
3. 360	8. 1970
4. 1964	9. 1932
5. 2006	10. 1944

```
1 1 9 8 7 4 0 7 1 1 3 4
2 3 9 1 3 2 8 5 8 1 0 1
8 1 9 8 4 0 4 2 6 7 1 9
9 8 7 4 5 1 2 3 1 9 8 1
1 8 9 4 0 9 6 6 0 1 9 8
1 9 4 4 7 9 2 0 1 4 3 0
9 1 4 5 8 0 9 6 7 7 7 1
7 4 0 3 5 8 1 9 6 4 2 9
0 6 0 0 2 8 3 6 5 0 1 0
```

SOCIAL STUDIES, page 76

1. Social Security
2. American Samoa
3. Ginsburg
4. Sri Lanka
5. Humanities
6. Subway
7. Andorra
8. Carter
9. Homeland Security
10. Apollo

Phrase: Social Studies rocks!

WORLD AND WEATHER, page 104

Here are the "out of place" words and the list topics:

1. Vancouver, High U.S. Mountains
2. Moses, Top Mountain Climbers
3. Palau, Smallest Countries by Size
4. New Orleans, Smoggiest U.S. Cities
5. Alaska, Most Visited States
6. Miami, Active Volcanoes
7. Al-Aqsa, Driest Places
8. Gordon, People Who Went Around the World (last names)
9. Peanut, U.S. Cities Named for Food
10. Corks, Names of Seashells

SCIENCE, page 136

Here are the 10 "quadruple matches."

Andromeda, Astronomy, Atlantis, 1985
Element, Chemistry, Gas, 115
Deca, Math, Power, 10,000
Stratum corneum, Dermatology, Dermis, 5
Incisors, Dentistry, Canine, 32
Ethanol, Power, Corn, GS450
Cloning, DNA, Sheep, 1996
Solar cells, Electricity, Power, 0.3
CAT, Tomography, Doctor, 3-D
Eucalyptus, Botanic, Specimen, 435

WORDS, page 168

E	N	D	R	U	N			
H		I			I	S		
E		C			G			C
A		T			H			A
D	E	F	I	N	I	T	I	O	N
		O						
I		N						R
F	R	A	N	K	E	N	F	O	O	D
		R						O
G	Y	M	N	A	S	I	U	M

POP CULTURE, page 196

Jennifer Aniston
Ice Cube
Mario Brothers
Maxwell Smart
Neville Longbottom
Elvis Presley
Usher
Tiki Barber
Ralph Wiggum
Oprah Winfrey
Nemo

Answer: Jimmy Neutron

ANIMALS, page 224

1. deer
2. rhino
3. ostrich
4. hermit crab
5. bison
6. narwhal
7. lab rat
8. tetra
9. arachnid

Secret animals: human beings

FOOD, page 248

The mixed up meal is
Chicken
Asparagus
Mashed Potatoes
Milk
Cheesecake

GRAB BAG, page 276

1. vomitologist
2. Wat Pho Buddha
3. Conor
4. A. Janus; B. Sunne; C. Emperor;
   D. Roman

Mystery word: humectant

SPORTS, page 308

Signing Off

At the end of TV programs — mostly news shows, but some fictional shows — the hosts or newscasters often used well-known phrases to say good-bye or good night. They each created catchphrases that have stood the test of time (mostly!). Here are some famous "sign-offs" from TV history (plus one movie). And now . . . it's our turn to sign off. We'll just use "See ya later, alligator!"

"And that's the way it is."
—Walter Cronkite, CBS News

"Good night and good news."
—Ted Baxter (Ted Knight) on *The Mary Tyler Moore Show*

"For now, Dick Clark—so long."
—Dick Clark on *American Bandstand*

"See you on the radio."
—Charles Osgood, *CBS This Morning*

"Good night and good luck."
—Edward R. Murrow on radio and TV

"And so it goes."
—Linda Ellerbee on *NickNews*

"Seacrest . . . out!"
—Ryan Seacrest on *American Idol*
(though it didn't last long as a sign-off!)

"Stay classy, San Diego."
—Ron Burgundy (Will Ferrell) in *Anchorman*

The comic team of George Burns and Gracie Allen had a great sign-off. Allen's character was, well, not too bright. At the end of their shows, Burns would say, "Say good night, Gracie." And she'd say, "Good night, Gracie!"